The Way W...

*Gay and lesbian lives in the
21st century*

Edited by

Ben Summerskill

continuum
LONDON • NEW YORK

Continuum

The Tower Building	80 Maiden Lane, Suite 704
11 York Road	New York
London SE1 7NX	NY 10038

www.continuumbooks.com

The Publisher wishes to thank Mark Bostridge who had the original idea for the book and Joe Galliano at *Gay Times* for helpful discussions at the early stages of this project. The Editor wishes to thank Peter Knight at Stonewall.

First published 2006

British Library Cataloguing-in-Publication Data
A catalogue record for this book is available from the British Library.

ISBN 0–8264–8785–8

Typeset by Kenneth Burnley, Wirral, Cheshire
Printed and bound by Antony Rowe Ltd

Contents

Notes on contributors

Jane Czyzselska has written for *DIVA* since 1994, and became editor on April Fool's Day 2004. An auspicious day for her (it's her mum's birthday), she waved her freelance career as a journalist for *The Times*, the *Independent* and *Horse & Hound* goodbye. She loves: mongrels, dj-ing in a 'Can't mix, won't mix' style (Olivia Newton John's 'Hopelessly Devoted To You' sounds perfect after My Bloody Valentine's 'Sunny Sundae Smile'), afternoon naps and Brigitte Bardot in *The Wicker Man*. She hates: not being able to speak Spanish.

Antony Sher was born in South Africa. For the last 30 years he has lived in Britain, where he is established as one of the country's leading actors and a successful writer and artist. His novels are the highly acclaimed *Middlepost* (1988), *The Indoor Boy* (1991), *Cheap Lives* (1995) and *The Feast* (1998). His other works include the theatre journals *Year of the King* and *Woza Shakespeare!* (co-written with his partner, the theatre director Gregory Doran), *Primo Time* (2004), and a collection of his paintings and drawings, *Characters*. The first volume of his autobiography *Beside Myself* was published in 2001. His stage play *I.D.* was performed at the Almeida Theatre in September 2003, and his adaptation of *If This Is a Man* by Primo Levi was performed at the Royal National Theatre in autumn 2004 and in New York in summer 2005. He is an Associate Artist of the Royal Shakespeare Company. In 2000, he was knighted for his services to acting and writing.

Tony Peake has contributed to four volumes of *Winter's Tales*, *The Penguin Book of Contemporary South African Short Stories*, *The Mammoth Book of Gay Short Stories* and *Seduction*, a themed anthology which he also edited. He is the author of two novels, *A Summer Tide* (1993) and *Son to the Father* (1995), and the biography *Derek Jarman* (1999).

Stella Duffy has written ten novels. *State of Happiness* (2004) was long-listed for the 2004 Orange Prize, and is in development with Fiesta Productions for whom she is also writing the screenplay. She was co-editor of the anthology *Tart Noir*, from which her story 'Martha Grace' won the 2002 CWA Short Story Award. She has written over 25 stories and many feature articles. With the National Youth Theatre she adapted her novel *Immaculate Conceit* for the Lyric Hammersmith, most recently writing and directing *Cell Sell* for the NYT at the Soho Theatre. She also writes and performs for radio. Stella was born in south London, grew up in New Zealand, and has lived in the UK since 1986. She is married to the writer Shelley Silas.

Craig Jones joined the Royal Navy in 1989. He qualified as a Heli-copter Fast Rope Instructor in 1991, undertaking air-launched drug enforcement boarding in the Caribbean in 1991 and UNSCR boarding in the Northern Arabian Gulf in 1992. In 1993 he was appointed as Executive Officer of HMS *Itchen* patrolling the coastal borders of Northern Ireland. With his Royal Marine troop he under-took armed counter-terrorist boarding and beach-mounted vehicle checkpoints in the difficult times immediately before the ceasefire. He has served on HMS *Illustrious*, HMS *Invincible* and HMS *Fearless*. In addition to his warfare duties, he is principal consultant to the Ministry of Defence and the Royal Navy on gay and lesbian issues in the Armed Forces and was awarded an MBE in the 2006 New Year Honours in recognition of his contribution to Equality and Diversity in the Armed Forces. Craig lives with his partner Adam in Brighton.

Irshad Manji is a Canadian author, journalist and activist. A Muslim by birth and faith, she is also an outspoken lesbian, feminist and critic of Islamic fundamentalism. She was once described by the *New York Times* as 'Osama bin Laden's worst nightmare'. She is the author of the bestselling book *The Trouble with Islam*. Between 1998 and 2001 she was the host and senior producer of *Q Files* on Citytv. She was also the host and producer of *In the Public Interest* on Vision TV, and was involved in the televised debate series *Friendly Fire*. Manji is the current President of VERB, a Canadian channel aimed at young people and specializing in diversity. She hosts the *Big Ideas* programme on TVOntario, and is a writer-in-residence at the University of Toronto Hart House. Manji was awarded Oprah Winfrey's first annual Chutzpah Award for 'audacity, nerve, boldness and conviction'. She is also a recipient of the Simon Wiesenthal Award of Valor.

Matthew Parris worked for the British Foreign Office from 1974 to 1976. From 1976 to 1979 he worked in the Conservative Party Research Department, and was Conservative MP for West Derbyshire from 1979 to 1986. He was the presenter for the London Weekend Television series *Weekend World* from 1986 to 1988. Matthew is a freelance journalist and broadcaster, and a columnist for *The Times*.

Sarah Weir is Executive Director, Arts Council London. She was previously at the Almeida Theatre where she had been Executive Director since January 2001. Sarah started her career with 15 years in the Lloyd's insurance market. She worked for Aldgate Group Brokers, where she rose to become their Non-Marine Managing Director. Following a change of career from business into the arts and a year working at Purdy Hicks Gallery, Sarah moved to the Association of Business Sponsorship of the Arts (now Arts and Business) as Head of their Pairing Scheme. She also completed a part-time History of Art BA at Birkbeck College. In 1997, Sarah moved to the Royal Academy of Arts as Head of Corporate Sponsorship and then became Fundraising Director in 1999.

David Starkey According to the *Daily Mail*, Starkey is 'the rudest man in Britain'. He is a leading commentator on the state of British politics and leadership throughout the ages and society. He appears frequently on television and radio. David is a respected academic, his research interests having developed to include a broad spectrum of cultural, social and political history. He has written or edited several books, including *Rivals in Power, The Reign of Henry VIII: Personalities and Politics, The English Court from the Wars of the Roses to the Civil War,* and *Elizabeth: Apprenticeship* which has been rated the number one non-fiction bestseller in *The Times*. The book accompanies his series *Queen Elizabeth I* screened on Channel 4 which achieved the highest-ever rating for a history programme shown on that channel and followed the huge success of his previous series *King Henry VIII*.

Brian Paddick is Deputy Assistant Commissioner of the Metropolitan Police Service, and is responsible for the day-to-day delivery of routine policing services across London, from the response to emergency calls to the investigation of some serious offences including rape and attempted murder. Brian is known for his innovative approaches to policing, which some have described as 'radical' but which he describes as 'pragmatic'. He studied Politics, Philosophy and Economics at Queen's College, Oxford and Business Administration at Warwick Business School.

Stewart Brown joined the fire service when he was 19. He is an Executive Council Member of the Fire Brigade Union where he represents gay and lesbian firefighters on the gay and lesbian committee.

Maggi Hambling has dedicated her turbulent and unconventional life to a 'selfish business' – her work. She is a figurative painter, sculptor and printmaker whose exuberant presence has enlivened the British art world for over 20 years. She was the First Artist in Residence at the National Gallery, London (1980–81). Her paintings have been collected by many museums including the Tate Gallery, National Gallery and the National Portrait Gallery. Her acclaimed public statue of Oscar Wilde was unveiled next to Trafalgar Square in 1998. She is proud to have been once banned from the Gateways, a lesbian club in Chelsea, for suggestive dancing.

Alan Hollinghurst is author of four novels: *The Swimming Pool Library* (1988), *The Folding Star* (1994), *The Spell* (1998) and *The Line of Beauty* (2004), which was awarded the 2004 Man Booker Prize.

Rashida X is the Chairperson of Imaan, the social support group for British Lesbian, Gay, Bisexual and Transgender Muslims. Imaan was founded in September 1998 in London. They hold monthly meetings in central London, have held three conferences welcoming people from as far away as the US and Canada to Israel and Malaysia. They also make special arrangements for Islamic festivals like Ramadan and Eid. Imaan has a membership of about 250 people. Rashida X has written for *DIVA* magazine, *The Guardian* and *Gay Times* about gay Muslim issues.

Damon Galgut is a novelist living in Cape Town. He was born in Pretoria in 1963. His latest novel, *The Good Doctor* (2003), set in post-apartheid South Africa, explores the uneasy friendship between two very different men in a deserted, rural hospital. It was shortlisted for the 2003 Man Booker Prize for Fiction. *The Good Doctor* has been translated into 16 languages.

Robert Taylor took up photography after serving in the Royal Air Force, qualifying as a barrister and several eventful years in educational book publishing in Nigeria and the UK. He has been exhibited and published widely. His work is held in the National Portrait Gallery, the Victoria & Albert Museum and several private collections. His current projects include an exploration of contemporary arts in Slovakia, and reform in UK prisons.

V. G. Lee has written three novels: *The Comedienne* and *The Woman in Beige* published by Diva Books and *Diary of a Provincial Lesbian*, published in 2006 by Onlywomen Press. She is also a poet and a freelance creative writing tutor.

Daniel Harbour is a writer based in London. His book *An Intelligent Person's Guide to Atheism* was published in 2001.

Helen Munro is Director of a consultancy specializing in public and parliamentary affairs. With a background in social policy, Helen leads on accounts in the education, environmental protection and the charitable sector. Helen is also an 'enthusiastic' footballer.

Stephen Hough is an internationally acclaimed concert pianist and a composer. Since winning first prize in the Naumburg International Piano Competition in 1983 he has appeared regularly with most of the major American orchestras and with numerous European orchestras under conductors including Abbado, Ashkenazy, Dohnányi, Dutoit, Gergiev, Järvi, Levine, Maazel, Oramo, Rattle, Salonen, Slatkin, Tilson Thomas and Vanska. He has had numerous original compositions and transcriptions published by Josef Weinberger Ltd.

Credit: Piers Allardyce

Introduction

Ben Summerskill

In the 1980s, we had answerphones so we could pretend to be in when we were out. Two decades later, we have answerphones so we can pretend to be out when we're in. Similar social changes, some small but all meaningful, seem to have transfigured the lives of Britain's four million gay people in the same period.

For them, Christmas came early in 2005. Arrival of civil partnership enabled them to give notice that they intended to register their partnerships at town halls from early December. A fortnight later, lesbian and gay couples were exchanging 'I dos' for the first time, not just in registry offices but – in happy harmony with the way we live now – in the stately homes of down-at-heel aristocrats and below deck on HMS *Belfast* too.

For inhabitants of the Westminster beltway, life for gay people might appear to have changed completely in recent years. Since the summer of 2003, four major gay legislative demands have secured passage through a doggedly traditional House of Lords.

If you were only a political lobbyist, twenty-first-century Britain might seem the bravest of new worlds: repeal of the notorious Section 28 of the Local Government Act, which ridiculously forbade the so-called 'promotion of homosexuality'; aggravated sentences for hate crimes against gay people; and protection against discrimination in the provision of goods and services. All were conceded by gay-sceptic peers between 2003 and 2005.

The change is poles apart from the current experience of gay people in America. During a bitterly fought 2004 presidential election, the issue of gay marriage – with flames fanned both by gay activists and by their evangelical Christian detractors – demonstrated a capacity to invest the political domain with an unusual poison.

And even Britain's latest legislative hurly-burly is in stark contrast to the one change – on lesbian and gay adoption – that peers had previously grudgingly conceded since the election of a Labour government in 1997. As recently as the late 1990s, the former deputy leader of the Conservatives in the Lords, evangelical Christian Baroness Blatch, could get away with hissing loudly upon espying Lord Alli, then the only gay peer: 'Don't you know he's queer as the Ace of Spades?'

Civil partnership itself, for which Stonewall and others campaigned so hard, is transformative. It offers gay people every single right, and responsibility, invested in marriage. Even the Slaughterhouse Act 1974 has been assiduously amended by owlish civil servants so that a lesbian might bequeath a slaughterhouse licence to her partner (should the happy couple happen to own an abattoir, of course).

Gay people no longer risk resentful families preventing them attending a hospital bedside. And hundreds of thousands of public sector workers are now entitled to leave a survivor pension to their partner, something they have been disgracefully forced to fund in the past without ever having the opportunity to pass on the benefit of their labours.

In December 2005, the *Economist* acknowledged that British civil partnership would soon be dubbed 'gay marriage'. And 'Elton and David get wed' headlines in tabloid papers – and possibly even posher 'compact' ones too – now reach millions who once doggedly claimed they had never known of anyone who was homosexual.

Civil partnership has also opened a hitherto unexplored world to many gay couples. *Stag and Groom* magazine, one of the successes of 'niche publishing' in recent years, features a bewildering – for many gay people – introduction to stag night etiquette, orders of service and wedding day hosiery. A recent edition offered pictorial hints about how to carry your bride over the threshold. The piece was headlined: 'Levitate, don't herniate'.

For many gay people, partnership recognition has been distinctly different from other welcome legal changes such as equalizing the age of consent, for it has meant practical changes to the lives of millions of heterosexuals too. For the first time, Auntie Maureen and Uncle Fred have been invited to their gay nephew's wedding reception.

This all represents a world-class challenge to the 'hetero-normativity' bemoaned by po-faced sociologists in university common rooms for 30 years. For while Britain's wider population might have disobligingly resisted academic entreaties to challenge their own 'hetero-normativity', they do fully understand that if their cousin, son, auntie or schoolmate wants to have a wedding list at Debenhams and a honeymoon in the Maldives, it makes them pretty much the same as everyone else.

Most important of all, the introduction of civil partnership gave the message to a generation of young lesbians and gay men, and will give one to generations to come, that when they grow up they will be entitled to the same respect and fair treatment as their heterosexual counterparts.

A tart corrective to the idea popular among some liberal intelligentsia that Britain has completely changed for the better as far as 'gay stuff' goes was the killing of Jody Dobrowski on south London's Clapham Common in October 2005. Still too shy and embarrassed even to visit a gay bar, the 24-year-old was kicked to a slow death to reported chants of homophobic abuse.

Campaigners at Stonewall are only too well aware that changing the law, tough though it might be, is really just the easy part. Changing the world is tougher still. And if you remain unconvinced that there's still a problem, just visit any school playground in Britain. The insult 'gay' is in common usage, even in primary schools.

Three out of four bullied lesbian and gay young people say they feign illness or play truant to escape school bullying, and one in four secondary school teachers say they are aware of physical homophobic bullying.

It's almost a decade since a British Labour government pledged that 'education, education, education' would be at the heart of its programme because bad schooling compromised children's life chances for ever. Yet lesbian and gay 16-year-olds with good GCSE results are more likely to leave school than their heterosexual counterparts, something which compromises their life chances for ever too. Although many schools take some sorts of bullying seriously, other forms may be less of a priority. In a secondary school in the West Country last year, a group of final year students finally tired of racist graffiti which had adorned a school corridor for months. One morning, they brought brushes and paint to school – and painted over the graffiti with the words 'Glad to be gay'. The head teacher had the corridor redecorated within 24 hours.

Confidence that homophobic bullying will be effectively addressed is scarcely enhanced by the knowledge that Ruth Kelly, the cabinet minister put in charge of our schools in 2004, had recently voted against equality for gay people.

Britain's National Health Service was legendarily created by a Labour government to be free at point of delivery to all. Yet many lesbian and gay patients still receive treatment that could only be described as second class in a fit of generosity.

Recent research carried out for the NHS in Scotland sourced details of cases including a gay man referred by the NHS at public expense to a Christian-based counselling centre. He was humiliatingly told he would not recover from his alcohol dependency unless he 'gave up' homosexuality.

In east London, in a case which is not isolated, a gay man was declined treatment by his Muslim NHS GP after disclosing his sexual orientation. In south Wales, in a similarly unexceptional episode, a woman was refused a smear test on the declared grounds that she was lesbian.

Individual cases such as these led Stonewall to start investigating the prevalence of exclusion of gay people from mainstream health care in 2005. In Brighton, only three in five of a sample of almost 300 women had had smear tests; the figure is four in five for women in the wider population.

In the media too, lesbians and gay men remain almost invisible. And when they do crop up, as *EastEnders* demonstrated in late 2005, it's as lurid stereotypes. The BBC1 soap might have made groundbreaking history almost two decades ago when Colin pecked Barry on the cheek. But sensible Sonia's innocent peck from Naomi apparently left Sonia so traumatized that she instantly jumped into bed with her virtually estranged vegetable of a husband. It would warm the cockles of prudish BBC founder Lord Reith's heart.

While some soap operas might move with the times, *EastEnders* appears to delight in regressing. Its last gay visitor, from 2001 to 2005, was Derek. The actor Ian Lavender, who played him, remains much better remembered for appearing as Private Pike in the comedy *Dad's Army* 30 years earlier.

To satisfy the prudes who appear to run BBC1 nowadays, *EastEnders'* Derek had almost no human characterization at all. In his long tenure in Albert Square, whose other residents seem to rival the Bloomsbury Group as bedhoppers, viewers never benefited from a single meaningful insight into Derek's current private life. He arrived as producer of a panto (a touchingly dull stereotype) and the only evidence ever disclosed of passion in his past was when he once had a – touch-free – chance meeting with a former boyfriend. His ex turned out to be an entertainments manager in a holiday camp. You couldn't make it up, as the Redcoats say.

Lord Reith might well have approved. But his successors 70 years later might just be underestimating the British – and the worldwide – public. In 1994, publisher Secker & Warburg released a new novel by Louis de Bernières. At point of publication the book received little acclaim. It received almost no notice whatsoever in the literary pages of the national newspapers which make or break bestsellers. Who knows why a book with not one but five chapters entitled 'The Homosexual' didn't endear itself to those who often judge popular taste so well?

The homosexual of de Bernières' creation was Carlo, a tough, devoted, kind, soldierly and brave hero of exactly the sort that doesn't feature in the wider popular imagination. Yet, in spite of this atypical figure at the heart of its narrative, *Captain Corelli's Mandolin* went on to become a worldwide bestseller, making de Bernières himself a multimillionaire.

It is instructive – although perhaps not yet to enough fashionable media folk – that when John Madden went on to turn the novel into a highly promoted film starring Nicolas Cage and Penelope Cruz in 2001, all references to Carlo's homosexuality were ruthlessly exorcized. What had been a nuanced narrative was turned – in spite of the stunning cinematic backdrop of Cephalonia – into a workaday study of human emotions in little more than black and white. And the film bombed. Perhaps its producers might rather more profitably have trusted the maturity of worldwide audiences.

In 2005 and 2006, those audiences embraced a startlingly romantic new film by director Ang Lee. The protagonists in *Brokeback Mountain*, set in 1963, were a Wyoming ranch hand and a rodeo cowboy who fall in love. It's hardly surprising that the movie has secured a cult following given that, for many gay people, it will have been the first time they have ever seen their ordinary lives represented in cinema. (Heterosexuals who struggle with understanding how gay people feel about their invisibility in the media might reflect upon how they would themselves feel if they had spent a lifetime of school and university education never once reading a set text which featured a heterosexual character.)

Lord Reith would undoubtedly take comfort from the noisy opposition to gay equality still coming from some parts of the British establishment. To mark the introduction of civil partnership in Britain, the *Daily Telegraph* duly featured a bitter polemic from 'Why-oh-Why' columnist Ferdinand Mount. He derided 'startling progress for a way of life which was illegal well within living memory and which has just been condemned by Pope Benedict as "intrinsically disordered"'. Ferdie's principal practical complaint seemed to be about the Islington Council registrar who would soon host a ceremony between actor Sir Antony Sher and his partner, a director with the Royal Shakespeare Company. Shockingly, to Ferdie Mount if to no one else, she was exactly the same one who had recently married Ferdie's beloved daughter. (No doubt there were also *Telegraph* columnists in the 1960s who similarly bemoaned the fact that their Martini glass at the Savoy might recently have been used by a black man.)

Standing shoulder to shoulder alongside Mr Mount is the *Daily Mail's* Melanie Phillips. With her trademark cropped hair and brusque manner, she is one of the trenchant campaigners for 'family values' who seem – distressingly for so many – to have lost the argument. The Office of National Statistics reported recently that it expected the number of unmarried people in Britain to outnumber the married for the first time by 2030.

But heterosexuals themselves don't necessarily make very good advertisements for marriage. As a tabloid journalist, thoughtful Melanie is presumably well acquainted with the personal excitements of pop singer Britney Spears. Britney was for many years a pin-up of social conservatives worldwide as an exemplar of their beloved abstinence before marriage. Even George Bush cited the singer as a role model for American youth.

In 2004 the star – who had actually been having intimate relations with fellow popster Justin Timberlake while being fêted against her will as a teen-virgin – did demonstrate a devotion to marriage of a sort, by getting heroically drunk late one night and marrying a casual acquaintance – not actually Mr Timberlake – in a Las Vegas wedding chapel. Britney demonstrated an equally heroic penitence by securing an annulment as soon as her hangover had worn off two days later.

Espying these loose morals celebrated across the pages of the organs which pay their lavish salaries, Mel, Ferdie and their pals must weep. But too often they give the regrettable impression that, in their frustrated despair at losing the argument for the sanctity of marriage, they are happy to give a good kicking to a small minority group – of gay people – who were never going to get married in the first place.

A nation's treatment of its gay citizens can be a touchstone of democracy. In 1995, Zimbabwean President Robert Mugabe denounced homosexuals in inflammatory language. They were lower than pigs and dogs and deserved to be attacked in the streets. The international near-silence, except from some diligent gay campaigners, was arresting. Newspapers, trades unionists and progressive politicians worldwide might have taken the opportunity to condemn an exercise in blatant hatemongering. Just over a decade later, Mugabe had come for the newspapers and for the trades unionists and for the opposition politicians too – just as the Nazis did for the compliant Pastor Niemoller 65 years earlier. And now there is no one left to speak up for them.

Similar human rights outrages against gay people in Iran, Dubai and Turkey are reported today with distressing regularity, but they remain unchallenged. Even Tony Blair happily endorses the delights of holidaying in Egypt each Christmas. In an evident blind spot for a man who has helped deliver equality in many areas for gay people, he and his wife seem apparently oblivious to the country's routine detention of gay people for committing the crime of association.

The Church of England struggles similarly with the gay issue, happy to offer kind homilies, but failing to offer leadership. The Archbishop of Canterbury shared the view privately with a friend in 2005 that he sleeps soundly at night while his communion risks being rent asunder over homosexuality because 'someone bigger than all of us' is ultimately in charge. It's a pity that 'someone bigger than all of us' isn't himself in a position to point out that Peter Akinole, the Archbishop of Nigeria currently promoting schism within the Anglican Church, seems to have all too little to say about polygamy and female genital mutilation in his own country while cheerily condemning as 'satanic' the decision of his co-religionists to elect the gay Gene Robinson a Bishop in New Hampshire.

It is against this backdrop, of increasing individual freedom but sometimes achingly slow progress, that the lives detailed in this book are lived. Matthew Parris may see little prejudice in his everyday life, but Jane Czyzselska finds hate on our streets.

Most lesbians and gay men celebrate the transformation they have seen in their lifetimes not least because not to do so would be graceless to a legion of friends who have helped secure it, as Stella Duffy writes too. That doesn't deny a recognition that stubborn homophobia still blights all too many human lives, a fact of modern life confirmed starkly by the murder of Jody Dobrowski. Neither does it deny an increasing awareness that the poison planted in the minds of people such as those who killed Dobrowski is validated by expressions of disdain from all too many who still claim – improbably – to 'love the sinner but hate the sin'.

The columnists, clerics and small-c conservatives may bark, but the caravan of twenty-first-century Britain moves on. One felicitous outcome of Stonewall's campaign for civil partnership has been the message it has given to a government all too often overanxious about social reform. The roof has not fallen in, politically or socially. And it won't fall in any time soon.

Happily the same view is being taken every day too in the twenty-first century by lesbian and gay Britons choosing for the first time to unshackle themselves from the tyranny of the closet and come out as who they are.

For while politicians and so-called faith leaders might fret about an orgiastic decline in traditional values, the real world changes. Just look at the *Sun* newspaper. Progeny of the media empire which includes Fox and Sky News, the *Sun* has one of the largest circulations in the world. In spite of the political stable from which it hails, it has an acute – if commercially motivated – ability to demonstrate sensitivity to the minds of its millions of readers. That's why it backed the Labour Party in their landslide 1997 election campaign, entirely alive to what voters were going to do anyway.

And how did the *Sun*, which even ten years ago would have lampooned gay weddings, welcome news that Sir Elton John and his partner David Furnish intended to get hitched? With an adulatory editorial claming that the event would 'lend a touch of stardust' to civil partnership. Its headline? 'Gay Pride'. For many gay people, it is a more telling cultural weathervane than almost any other of the way we are now.

Jane Czyzselska

It's 11 p.m. at the GAY underground bar on Old Compton Street in November 2005 and a group of young stiletto-sharp lesbians are discussing the merits of a table of pretty girls who look as though they've just finished their maths homework. 'I tell ya, I could work that bitch. Look at her titties man. Fierce!' 'Yeah, but not before I got my hands on her, you loser' another retorts, smoothing down her denim miniskirt as she casts a lustful eye across the room.

It's a far cry from the bar-room banter I first came across as a lesbian freshman in the late 1980s. Back then, I was studying in Leeds, arguably the front-line of radical lesbian separatism. Lesbian separatists in their trademark frumpy weeds and rats-tail hair-don'ts roamed the streets in the northern quarter, keeping a close watch on women who wore so-called 'suspect Nazi' gear – ergo black leather trousers and jackets. 'Wimmin only' discos were organized at the North Leeds Trades Club, a venue popular among Left-leaning organizations and suffused with all the sexual promise of a church vestry at teatime.

At the entry desk the punters, many of whom had come from former pit villages and mining towns, would often find hand-written signs that read 'No SM or fascist gear', 'Dress to impress not oppress'. Denim and cheesecloth, linen and cotton were acceptable fabrics; leather and rubber, according to the self-appointed lesbian guardians, were not. On one occasion, the local police were called in to eject a woman who was considered a liability because she refused to peel off her leather motorbike jacket. The Sapphic sisters feared that her presence might be threatening to some of the fairer sex present.

Back then, the lesbian community was gripped by two major debates about how we should lead our sex lives: should we sleep with women for political rather than sexual preference because men – monsters all, natch – were the enemies of radical lesbian feminism? And while we did our best not to objectify our lovers, what was the politically correct way to conduct ourselves between the sheets? Dildos were a no-no among the vanilla Pollyanna-ish lesbians – the wearing of a phallus was considered an inappropriate mirroring of heterosexual sex, and S&M was frankly perverted; its ritualized powerplay apparently too close to the patriarchal gender war.

Or so the argument ran from the vanilla champions, led by Linda Bellos – black lesbian leader of London's Lambeth Council and one of the original so-called loony lefties – when she defended her position against the leather-clad, swastika-toting (and Jewish!) S&M devotees at the women's centre in Wild Court, London in 1988. I considered myself neither one nor the other but felt reluctant to go along with the policing of private, consensual sexual acts.

'Lesbian culture in the 1980s was in its teenage years,' claimed the iconoclastic American academic Camille Paglia, the bête noir of many British lesbians and feminists. Her assertion that lesbians would benefit from sleeping with men, at least once, and that lesbian culture was immature was the proverbial red rag to the bulldagger (that's hardcore butch for readers under the age of 25). And while her first assertion may have been typical of her agitational approach, her observation on the embryonic state of lesbian identity was spot on.

After all, until 1993, when mad, sexy Beth snogged plain, pale nanny Margaret on Channel 4's controversial soap, *Brookside*, lesbians had appeared on the telly about as often as a solar eclipse. Sure, we had *Prisoner Cell Block H* and if you squinted hard enough you could just about imagine seeing PC Juliet Bravo down your local lesbian club, but regular signs of lesbian life on the big or small screen were limited both in terms of frequency and variety. Lesbians had few role models, few media mirrors to reflect their existence. Lesbians quite literally had no face.

In 1993, I was working by day as the marketing manager of a fire alarm and emergency exit sign company in Dewsbury, aka lesbian purgatory. I was lucky enough to have discovered my first long-term girlfriend, and first love, Ruth, who looked like a cross between Linda Evangelista and Isabella Rossellini and worked as a staff trainer for The Body Shop. The gay scene in Leeds comprised four venues: a no-nonsense three-storey homosexual knocking shop called Rockshots, the monthly camper-than-thou Confettis and two pubs, The Bridge and New Penny, the northern homosexual variation on the traditional spit'n'sawdust hostelry. Ruth and I tried not to spill our lager and blackcurrant onto the cut-price Axminster in The Bridge as we booed the mysogynist drag acts. Minge'n'Packet were firm local favourites and their repertoire consisted almost entirely of lesbian-baiting jokes worthy of Bernard Manning.

I wasn't out at work yet and made use of a gay male friend with a BMW who passed as my boyfriend at the annual Christmas 'do' held at a mock-Tudor pub in neighbouring Batley. I made the bold move to out myself shortly after the receptionist expressed her disappointment at the arrest of serial killer (of gay men) Colin Ireland. 'That's a shame,' she complained, as she read the cover story of her red-top daily. 'Ee were doing a right good job of getting rid of them queers.'

Later that day, news had spread like bird flu round the canteen that there was a lesbian in their midst. As I tiptoed across the shop floor, the hum of voices stopped before a workmate ventured in to check whether the rumours were true. 'I hear you're a bit of a lesbian?' he said rhetorically. 'Oh, really?' I countered. 'And which bit would that be then? My right arm definitely is but I think my hips are still in denial.'

Soon after this episode, I felt my time as a gay standard-bearer in the location equivalent of the lesbian Antarctic must draw to a close. I had been writing a monthly, mouthy column for a local gay publication when I applied for and was offered an incredibly privileged position as deputy editor of a homosexual parish gazette known as *All Points North*. Privileged, I felt, because now I could be as gay as I liked without the raised eyebrows and covert sniggering of homophobic colleagues.

It was 1993 and ripples of excitement were spreading eastwards from America when torch and twang singer k d lang appeared alongside Cindy Crawford on the cover of *Vanity Fair* magazine. An article about 'lipstick lesbians' announced the emergence of a new breed of dyke who – shock – liked lady things such as make-up. As a long-time wearer of lipstick, I was asked to appear on a late-night talk show as a lipstick champion, interviewed by Derek Hatton, of Liverpool City Council and militant notoriety. Lesbians were still perceived by many men as a threat to their very existence, and, as a high-heel-wearing, curly-haired femme, I puzzled the hell out of a succession of men in previous workplaces who thought I was using my sexuality as a shield against their sexual advances.

It was around this time that I started running a gay nightclub, Glamourpussy. My girlfriend Ruth and I dressed in a range of outrageous, and mostly extremely feminine, clothes. On more than a few occasions our sexuality was called into question by some of the unreconstructed butches who often treated us no better than your typically sexist bloke.

As a reasonably attractive femme girl, I rarely came across the same kind of homophobia as my more 'masculine'-looking gay girlfriends. As director-performer, Lois Weaver observes, femmes didn't then and still don't experience homophobia as much as butches do, but we're the victims of sexism, rather. We're more likely to be eroticized, sexually harassed, diminished, belittled – not queer-bashed. We are easier to dismiss because we don't challenge the *status quo* like butches do – we don't challenge what it means to be a man, or men's prerogative, which is the root of homophobia.

Since I came out in 1987, I've lived with the threat of, rather than direct, homophobia – as far as I am aware. My CV didn't hide the fact that I had worked for gay publications and I'll never know if my applications for some of the positions I applied for fell flat at the first post because of someone's fear of or objection to lesbians. If I suffered on a personal level at all, it was at the level of self-esteem: because I was gay and gays were not perceived as equal to heterosexuals, I expected to be treated badly and so for many years I accepted low-paid jobs in the gay media, either as a staff writer or as a freelance.

It's an interesting conundrum that so many gay organizations have been staffed by an underpaid workforce – it's almost as if we are so desperate to work with other gays that we are prepared to take a pay cut to do so. Of course the other side to this situation is that gay media organizations, up until fairly recently, have been poorly funded due to a reluctance by major mainstream brands to associate with homosexuality. In 2004, when *DIVA*'s advertising team were cold-calling some of the major clothing and beauty retailers, they were met with the blanket response: 'Sorry but no, we're a family brand'.

By the late 1990s, as gay rights organizations such as Stonewall, Outrage and local groups around the country were becoming increasingly successful with their campaign work, gay and lesbian life at a public level was becoming more evident to gays and non-gays alike. By this time, the so-called pink pound had been identified and gay men in particular were being courted by a raft of 'progressive' businesses eager to cash in on the DINKY demographic.

On television – that most powerful of media – we were beginning to see more gay programming and another window on the 'everylesbian' psyche. *Queer as Folk* (1999) introduced us to Britain's first glamorous professional dyke couple Hazel and Donna. They were slightly more boyish – butch as softened out pageboy – and they were shown as a civilizing force amidst the hedonism and somewhat sex-obsessed gay male scene. Career women and homemakers Donna and Hazel wanted to co-parent with their club bunny pal Stuart. At a time when the gay lifestyle was presented as a cypher for an aspirational way of life, free from so-called burdens of traditional heterosexuality, this was an interesting positioning of lesbians. Concurrently, lesbian and gay content on any programme from this point on was often used as a signifier of hip modernity.

But compared with lesbian characters in American TV shows, lesbians on British telly have had a tendency to be 'issuized', perhaps unsurprisingly. We are the object and not the subject and there are few exceptions to this. One such exception is the rural soap opera *Emmerdale* where vet Zoe Tate is subject to the crazy ideas of the script writers as much as the next heterosexual character, and for all its depressing placing of the biggest group of lesbians – prior to *The L Word* – the cult lesbian series *Bad Girls* has consistently presented real, believable, flawed and arguably human lesbian characters.

Over the years, lesbians have grown up with an increasingly diverse range of lesbian characters in films: from Gina Gershon's lesbian action hero in *Bound* (1996) to Sophie Ward in *A Village Affair* (1994) where Ward's character Alice moves to the country with her boring hubby and ends up in the arms of a local lady villager, to Lisa Cholodenko's seductive and sophisticated – if drug-fucked – representation of lesbians in *High Art* (1998). Our lesbian images have reflected a partial, and often infuriatingly limited, picture of lesbians – the natural corollary of a comparatively minute cultural palette.

Throughout my time writing for the gay and mainstream media, I've noticed how lesbians have changed in relation to the images, services and options available to them. Where once we dragged our heels as we felt under-represented and unacknowledged, lesbians have swaggered into the new Millennium with a new confidence, certainly in the major urban areas of the UK. Outside the urban centres, where lesbian and gay people are better served and resourced, the changes are taking place more slowly.

Among a sea of ten or so gay male magazine titles, Britain still only has *DIVA* as its national glossy monthly and a handful of either free or small-print-run publications. Throughout its 11-year history, *DIVA* has charted the rise and rise of lesbian culture and in its new format is beginning to reflect a more mainstream, powerful and hip reflection of contemporary lesbian life. At *DIVA*, we don't hold up one icon of perfect lesbian identity: what's helpful is to give people a really wide range of ideals or images and not rely on just one person to wave the Sapphic flag. But we still need more lesbians to come out, whether in the public eye or whether it's the girl next door. In *DIVA* we have featured hip lesbian rap stars, successful pop and sports personalities, powerful civil servants and a couple of enterprising lesbians who set up a chocolate shop in Rutland. All are important because they are all role models in their own field.

Since 2000 we have seen Sue Perkins, Rhona Cameron, Clare Balding, Alex Parks, Clare Teal, Sandi Toksvig, MP Angela Eagle,

Channel 5 head honcho Dawn Airey, actresses Sophie Ward and Saffron Burrows come out in the UK. Previously we only had the Americans: Martina, Melissa Etheridge, kd lang, The Indigo Girls. And the US ranks of Sapphic role models have swelled to include actresses Cynthia Nixon, Portia di Rossi, Ellen, Rosie O'Donnell, sportswomen Rosie Jones and Sheryl Swopes. With the growing army of high-profile women who say that they'd 'do a girl' and the tabloid interest in 'bi-try' straight women, one could certainly say some of the stigma that has historically surrounded lesbianism has been diluted. Today being lesbian is no longer considered wrong, or a sign that a woman is not attractive enough to get a man or that she's a ball breaker. Yet the media men are still, in general, only prepared to run a lesbian story if it meets particular criteria.

In 2000 when I tried pitching a story about an Iranian lesbian fleeing the brutal Sharia Law where homosexuality is forbidden, the newsdesk of the liberal broadsheet I contacted was at pains to understand why it merited column inches. The young woman who had been refused asylum in the UK by then Home Secretary Jack Straw was facing almost certain death if she was returned to her home country. After I asked the straight male reporter to imagine living in a land where heterosexuality was punishable by death, he duly ran the story.

In 2005, most broadsheets are still reluctant to print stories about the lesbians from around the world who are fleeing persecution as a result of their sexuality. *DIVA* has tried to syndicate features on lesbian clergy and lesbians in the military who are fighting against fierce discrimination with little interest from the mainstream press. Yet in recent months, we have seen a growing number of *DIVA* exclusives picked up in the mainstream press. Our survey of the top university towns for lesbian undergraduates achieved a half-page lead story in *The Guardian* and many other local newspapers. A spread in the *Independent on Sunday* reported on the important, myth-busting findings of the Out Now 2005 *DIVA* and *Gay Times* Readers Survey: lesbians working full-time earn an average £24,783 per annum, a figure that is comfortably above the national average. Lesbians, it seems, have reached the place that gay men were at about five ago in terms of visibility. There really is a female pink pound, and certainly, as far as income is concerned, there are many lesbians who have cracked the glass ceiling.

While there is a sense that news-desks must now take more interest in lesbians, even if only to demonstrate their awareness of a growingly confident and demanding lesbian and gay population, in comparison to the focus on the stories about gay men, the public profile of lesbians is still wanting. One reason for this is that there are simply fewer women who identify as lesbian than men who identify as gay. This may be due to the fact that because women are allowed to be more fluid in their sexual expression than men, women are less likely to feel the need to use the term 'lesbian' and make it a life choice in the way that gay men do once they've crossed the fence. Paradoxically however it is, I believe, still easier to come out as a gay man than as a lesbian because of the sexism that all women face. I haven't yet come across the lesbian equivalent of the old (gay) boys' network but, as lesbian cartoonist Alison Bechdel observes: 'Because of the thawing of sexuality relations, I have noticed that women are coming out younger and younger, which is great because it eliminates all those tortured, wasted teenage years in the closet. It also decreases the likelihood that people will continue behaving like teenagers into their 20s, 30s and 40s, like my generation did. Or is still doing.'

Currently, some young women (and indeed older ones) have developed a problem with the words 'lesbian', 'dyke' etc., which is mainly cultural, in that they see these terms as describing a type (butch/ball-breaking feminist/unfashionable/stereotyped) that they don't identify with. Lesbianism has a bit of an image problem, not helped by the mainstream press, which still only seems to have two registers where gay women are concerned – over-sexed minx or frumpy old dyke. We are in a time of change, and young women are looking for new ways to identify themselves and their sexuality, which are meaningful to them. Lesbian culture is changing, but that's nothing new. What we're seeing now is just another shift, similar to what happened in the 1970s when the Women's Movement and lesbian-feminism had a huge impact on lesbian identity.

Because little is known about the lesbian market, many obvious advertisers have not yet courted this lucrative market. In recent years, Land Rover, HMV, Co-operative Bank, Swissair, ENO, Delta Airlines and Smart Bank have all placed adverts, but the more obvious travel companies, fashion and beauty houses haven't as yet been forthcoming. There's a prejudice hangover from the anti-feminist, anti-lesbian days of yore that some men in the advertising world would do well to cast off. In their parallel universe, lesbians apparently don't spend money, have no need for clothes, hair products, holidays, cars or fragrances.

So what else has changed? This morning when I went to my local newsagents, I overheard a group of schoolgirls jibing each other about being lesbian. 'Chi-chi gal fi dead,' said one, laughing as she munched on her crisps. But last night, I had a wonderful exchange when I sent flowers to a lover via Interflora. The first time I used Interflora to order a bouquet of flowers for a girlfriend in 1990, the telephone operator was audibly disgusted by the romantic words I asked to be written in the card. Fifteen years down the track, a similar call prompted the friendly Interflora employee to respond with a honeyed sigh: 'Aw that's lovely. It's so nice to hear when two people are in love.'

Antony Sher

One of my first memories is of falling in love with another boy. I was aged four-and-a-half, and we were in kindergarten together. My feelings for him were intense – much more than ordinary friendship – and somehow linked to his maleness, his male beauty; I remember light brown hair, tender eyes, a small, strong build. We were very close for a while, and then something happened, I don't know what, and we were separated. I remember a feeling of both loss and shame. This relationship had been 'wrong' I concluded, though I had no idea why.

It was a fitting introduction to the society in which I found myself – one of the most oppressive regimes of the last century – apartheid South Africa. Led by a group of brutal Christian fundamentalists – hardline Afrikaners of the Dutch Reformed faith – and with every aspect of life police-controlled, government-censored, it was a breeding ground for prejudice and intolerance. Racist, misogynist, anti-Semitic, homophobic. Since the last two categories applied to me, it's hardly surprising that I grew up with a profound sense of unease about my identity, especially my gayness. In the South Africa of my youth, the 1950s and 60s, a homosexual was known as a 'moffie'. The *Oxford Dictionary of South African English* suggests that this word was perhaps drawn from Afrikaans or Dutch slang, '*mofrodiet*' – hermaphrodite. When I heard it in childhood, it certainly seemed to refer to an alien, deformed creature, one to be both mocked and despised. As my sexuality woke into being, and I found myself increasingly attracted to other boys, I feared that I was one of these freakish moffies, and decided this was completely unacceptable. I entered adolescence and the closet at round about the same time. This was the first of my closets. When I moved to the UK in 1968, to attend drama school in London, I entered a second closet. I couldn't see any examples of famous Jewish actors, so I stopped admitting to my race (I had already stopped practising the religion). And then there was the third closet. White South Africans were hated here, so I started introducing myself as British. By now I was in so many closets I didn't know where the keys were any more, or which was which, or whether I could ever get out again.

It was complete lunacy of course – you can't deny who you are. Yet, oddly enough, there are two professions which encourage this deception: one is acting, the other is spying. For the first couple of years in my new country I was in complete disguise: I was a straight non-Jewish Englishman. How many people did I fool? Probably none. Certainly not the one who mattered most: me. I felt shallow, half-made, insubstantial. So now began the long process of battering down all those closet doors, emerging back into the daylight, and reconstructing who I actually was.

In terms of my gayness, I found it relatively easy to come out to my friends, much tougher to come out to my parents – though I was rewarded by their loving acceptance of the news – but the difficult one still lay ahead: coming out publicly. By now I was becoming established as an actor. I'd had a success on television – as the rampantly heterosexual Howard Kirk in *The History Man* – and even bigger successes in the theatre: as the title role in Shakespeare's *Richard III*, and as Arnold the drag queen in Harvey Fierstein's *Torch Song Trilogy*. Looking back, it seems ludicrous to have done *Torch Song* without coming out. Personally, it was a sadness – I rated the play highly, I was proud to be doing it – but nevertheless, as with all my other projects, I would ask the publicity people to brief journalists that I wouldn't discuss my private life. (What a giveaway that is!) At the time I probably justified this peculiar behaviour by claiming that an actor needed to be as anonymous as possible, to allow him to become other characters. Then two things happened to encourage me to take the next step, and come out publicly.

The first was my changing attitude to acting itself. I began my career by believing that the job was about concealing yourself – probably stemming from my own identity struggles – but now I was learning that it's the complete opposite. The acting I found myself admiring most was the kind where I could see the actor's soul. He or she may be playing Hamlet or Cleopatra, but what moved me was their own face, body, spirit.

The second factor in coming out was the shining examples provided by Ian McKellen and Simon Callow. At that time, I didn't know either of them personally, but I found their openness about their sexuality increasingly inspiring. How casually Simon Callow mentioned his gayness in his book *Being An Actor* – it was just commonplace, normal, it was just another fact about him – and how passionately Ian McKellen was involving himself in the politics of the gay movement. The acting profession was full of people like myself, who, although widely known to be gay, wouldn't say so out loud. This was just plain daft. The time had come to move, as it were, to the other camp.

I came out publicly in 1989, and like Simon Callow it was via a book – except mine was of paintings and drawings, *Characters* – and to my considerable surprise and ultimate amusement, I discovered that, after all my agonizing, no one took a blind bit of notice. Of course not. I'm not a celebrity. I'm primarily a theatre actor, and the story wasn't remotely newsworthy. Well, I say no one noticed, but there was an exception. Shortly after I had done the deed, the telephone rang and Ian McKellen was on the other end: 'Listen, we don't really know one another, I got your phone number from the RSC, hope you don't mind, but I just wanted to say one thing – thank you.'

I was touched by the gesture, and I understood it more with the passing of time. These days I am immensely heartened and, yes, grateful every time I see anyone come out, whether a celebrity or not. It does matter, every single one matters. And if the person in question has any access to the media at all, I think it's important to apply Simon Callow's witty and subversive principle: let's normalize our queer lifestyle. When I write my occasional travel pieces for *The Guardian* and *Sunday Times*, I always make a point of mentioning that I'm journeying with my partner Greg (Doran, Chief Associate Director of the RSC), exactly like a straight writer might mention that his wife or partner was on the trip. Just that, nothing more, nothing special. I like the idea that someone might be drawn to a piece in the travel pages because they are interested in a particular country, and along the way they absorb the fact that the narrator is gay, and they keep reading – hopefully.

In 1991 I gained a fresh perspective on the question of coming out publicly. The film-maker Derek Jarman had published an article in *The Guardian*, criticizing Ian McKellen for accepting a knighthood from Thatcher's government, which was certainly no friend to the gay movement; they were responsible for Clause 28. There was, however, a different argument to be put: it was significant that a right-wing government had honoured an openly gay man, and an activist, and McKellen would now be better placed to fight the cause from within the establishment. The playwright Martin Sherman and I decided to compose a letter in reply to Jarman, to ask members of the arts community to sign it, and to also publish it in *The Guardian*. Our list of names soon started to look very healthy; among the first to sign were Simon Callow, Stephen Fry, Cameron Macintosh, Alec McCowen, Ned Sherrin. I volunteered to try to recruit the film director John Schlesinger, but I wasn't hopeful. As friends, John and I had often discussed the question of coming out publicly, and he was adamant that he never would. In a way that was perhaps typical of his generation, he claimed that his gayness was in his work – referring to films like *Darling, Midnight Cowboy, Sunday Bloody Sunday* – and there was no need for him to broadcast it personally. Nevertheless I phoned him. As I finished reading the letter, he said breezily, 'Yes, all right, you can add my name.' I told him I was both pleased and surprised. What had happened to make him change his mind? 'Well, this is important,' he said, and then gave his laugh – a naughty bark of a laugh – adding, 'Anyway, I'm too old to care any more!'

We were less lucky in another, crucial area. We couldn't find any women who would sign. All the gay actresses I approached gave the same response: the profession was tougher for women than men, there were fewer parts, and they just couldn't risk it. We were getting worried. Could we seriously go to press with an all-male list? What signal would that give? Then one night I returned home to hear a joyous message on my answering machine: Martin Sherman singing out, 'We've got a lesbian, we have got a lesbian!' It was the actress Pam St Clement. Two other gay women were to follow – the playwright Bryony Lavery and the director Nancy Diuguid – but the final list was still predominantly male. I suspect – I hope – it might be different today.

I'm sometimes asked if coming out has damaged my own career, in terms of casting. Theatre, or certainly British theatre, is a mature and sophisticated arena in which I honestly don't believe that an actor's sexuality makes any difference to either producers or audiences. But what about screen casting? Has coming out affected my film and TV career? The simple answer is: coming out has been such a liberating and valuable thing, I truly don't care. The other answer is: I don't know. If I was out in 1980, at the time of *The History Man*, would the BBC have cast me as Howard Kirk, a modern-day Casanova? Possibly not. Certainly not if it was being made now, in an age when mainstream television seems to be run by little narrow-minded committees who believe there's a formula to art, a book of rules, a code which guarantees success. Before such a committee, if my name came up as a potential Howard Kirk, it would be automatically thrown out. For them, it would be a simple matter: the public wouldn't believe in Howard's compulsive womanizing if the actor was gay. Hollywood is even worse in this respect, challenging casting directors with the threat, 'The Mid-West will never buy it', which conjures up images of crazed rednecks lynching the local cinema projectionist if a faggot is in the movie. But here again, in the world of movies, Ian McKellen is achieving heroic things and taking groundbreaking steps. He is the first openly gay actor to be nominated for an Oscar. Sir Ian is leading the charge, and the rest of us must join the ranks, join the battle. And we must hope that movies and TV catch up with the modern world, that they grow up at last. In theatre we have a new phrase, 'colour blind', referring to the fact that black actors like Adrian Lester and David Oyelowo can now play Henry V and Henry VI without anyone minding, or even noticing. Let us look forward to the day when movie companies and TV stations become 'sexuality blind'.

On a personal level, I've been blessed. My relationship with Greg is 18 years old at the time of writing, in September 2005, and by 5 December a new Civil Partnership law will have come into being, allowing us to make our union official. As we have put on the invitation to the party, 'We're legal at last'. Far more important than the tax advantages will be gaining next-of-kin status. Everyone has heard those appalling stories of gay couples being separated by illness or accident: one partner is suddenly unconscious or dead and the other is denied access to the bedside or funeral. Greg and I are both embraced by the Sher and Doran families, so we are relatively confident this wouldn't happen to us

– though God knows what hostile bureaucratic systems might suddenly manifest themselves in hospitals and funeral parlours – but it's a vitally important landmark for the gay rights movement. Greg *is* my next-of-kin.

And what of those issues of identity which so troubled me as a young man? I only wish someone had told me earlier what valuable material lay buried in my mixture. Both as an actor and writer, the theme of the outsider is present in everything I do, and now I celebrate the fact that, as a gay Jewish white South African, I have virtually cornered the market in minority groups. For me there is only one question on this topic which remains unanswered. Who are the insiders? Where is this great herd of ordinary guys and gals from which we're excluded? I've never met them, I don't know them, I can't recognize them as part of the human species. We are complicated; we are a weird, beautiful, wise, stupid, vulnerable, dangerous form of life. 'Outsiders' simply learn to recognize this picture of humankind sooner than the rest.

Tony Peake

My eldest grandson, who is five and beginning to grapple with issues existential and social, is curious to know if his grandmother and I are, or ever were, married. His bewilderment is understandable. Grandmoo, as he calls her, lives with someone other than myself – her current husband, Keith – and I with Peter, for whom there is no convenient label, certainly not where an inquiring five-year-old is concerned.

But answer him I shall have to, if not now, then later, so I may as well start practising. And who knows? In the process I may even increase my own understanding of what has made me into such a curiosity – gay grandfather – while possibly also coming to a decision (since I'll be considering the nature of family relationships) as to whether or not I wish, after twenty years of cohabitation, to take advantage of recent legislation and register myself as Peter's civil partner. On many levels I find it wondrous that Peter and I are now, in a sense, finally free to 'marry'. Yet am I positive (given what I have experienced of marriage as an institution) that this is the fairy-tale ending I want for my story?

It's a story that begins, like many a fairy tale, in another time, another place: South Africa in the 1950s. The cosseted only child of elderly parents, I grew up near Johannesburg wanting one day to be a famous writer – 'more famous than Shakespeare' was how I optimistically expressed it. Packed off to boarding school at the tender age of seven (since my parents were elderly, and I an only child, they imagined they were doing me a favour by making me part of a 'bigger family'), it became my lonely habit at night, after I'd judged the others in my dormitory to be safely asleep, to arrange my sheets and blankets into a series of hills and valleys in order to flex my imagination by queening it over this invented landscape. Because yes, it was always as its queen, never its king, that I ruled my nocturnal realm.

Unlike my eldest grandchild, however, I didn't fuss unduly about gender, didn't see anything unusual in my choice of role. Besides, it wasn't very long before I was experimentally kissing my first girlfriend, and if I still found the hotly anticipated trips I occasionally took into the veld with a male friend to play doctors and doctors infinitely more thrilling and absorbing than playing doctors and nurses with my less exploratory girlfriend: well, I didn't dwell on the matter. Certain things had to remain unchallenged. For instance, that because my parents loved me so unreservedly, I must of course be careful never to disappoint them. To which end, being more famous than Shakespeare would go a long way; as would one day marrying and becoming a father, thereby ensuring the continuance of our family line.

Or perhaps I make too much of this? Perhaps what motivated me had less to do with parental expectation than with my sex drive, with how feverishly it excited me to cycle with my friend into the veld and unbutton his trousers and give myself over to the ensuing sensation of tight and tingling expectancy that can still, if I close my eyes, electrify me. Though because we are dealing with South Africa in the 1950s and 1960s, when the country was every bit as circumscribed sexually as it was politically – no such thing, in those days, as a gay role model – I didn't dare to think of further exploring other male bodies, of making this my emotional and sexual future. No matter how intense my secret longings, not once did I abandon having a girlfriend, or ever allow myself to imagine not marrying. To have done that would have been far more shocking than any trip into the veld.

And so, in due course, having inadvertently impregnated the woman I'd started going out with during my third year of university, marry is what I did; marry and become the proud father of two children, one boy, one girl. Prized and hard-won normality in all things – provided, of course, you exclude certain niggles, such as my parents' misgivings at the shotgun nature of my marriage. Or the Shakespeare fantasy, yet to be realized. Or, most crucially, the fact that here the fairy tale darkens, that now we enter a tangled wood prowled by a most disruptive wolf.

As a young man, I firmly believed that finding male bodies so thrilling was only skin-deep with me; a metaphoric boil, as it were, which, although recurring and troubling, could always be lanced. Whereas love, true love, emotional commitment as opposed to mere lust, was something I could experience only with a woman. And that I happened passionately to love my wife was never in question. True, we might argue bitterly; true, my eyes (even my hands) might on occasion wander; true, sometimes I felt sick to the stomach with worry (or fear, or uncertainty, or longing; I don't have the right word). But such passing confusion aside, Irene remained my necessary other half. Without her, I couldn't conceive of ever being whole; would always, I thought, be less than myself. Never mind the wonderful fact of our two children, the joy they brought, the sense of purpose, the contentment, the balance, the normality, the (yes) self-satisfaction.

By this stage, Irene and I had left South Africa and moved to London, where I encountered shops that openly sold magazines featuring naked men. Guiltily, I would buy these magazines, pore over them, then – in disgust, the boil lanced – destroy them. Until the fateful day when, on opening the case in which I kept my stash of magazines, I discovered a note from Irene asking which of the men I found the most titillating. So! My shameful secret was out! And to my surprise, once I'd overcome a surge of guilt, I experienced only relief. The closet door had begun to creak open, light had been cast on a previously darkened corner, what had before been solitary could suddenly be shared. Which indeed it was – enthusiastically so. Within weeks, the magazines had become something for us to enjoy together and, when we were out and about, Irene would frequently demand that I tell her if I spotted a particularly promising package. 'Crotch watching', we called it: a new and oh-so-sophisticated marital sport.

Self-deception is a strange thing; even as it blinds you to yourself, it encourages selfishness. At the time, I saw only my good fortune, the having of my cake and being able to eat it, an expression whose meaning, in any event, I'd never fully under-stood, since wasn't being able to eat your cake the whole point of having it? You didn't want merely to admire it, did you? What I steadfastly ignored, didn't even begin to comprehend, certainly not in relation to myself, was Irene's hurt; her growing insecurity; the rising desperation. Instead, I opted to view the fact that we had recently taken to luring an occasional man into bed with us as proof of how grown up we were, how able to accommodate our differences while celebrating our closeness. What could be more perfect, I asked myself, more bang-up-to-date, than the nuclear family that is able to dabble in fusion?

I mix my metaphors too hectically. But then Irene and I were a hectic, not to say combustible, mix – and the explosion, when it came, was devastating.

By this juncture, we were living in Spain, where the children could run free; where I could hopefully write; where all four of us might, we believed, more completely, more happily be ourselves. For Irene, this briefly meant falling in love with another man, which I took as sanction for me to step aside, which pitched Irene into despair. And so, in a welter of emotional confusion and con-tention, our marriage entered its lacerating final stages and a protracted process of unravelling began. Over the years, we had undertaken a series of moves (South Africa to London to Spain) in

the vain hope that geography might somehow solve what we ourselves couldn't. Now, by contrast, Irene elected, in the short term,
to remain in Spain with our children, while I packed my bags and
returned on my own to London.

There is more, of course, any number of degrading and distressing incidents, the detailing of which would take us so deep
into the wood that we'd never see light again. Suffice it to say that
one year later Irene had returned to England, found solace in the
arms of God, a more dependable source of support than I could
ever hope to be, and was living in Brighton with our daughter.
Our son, meanwhile, had come to live in London with me
because, given the state of virtual war then existing between Irene
and myself, I fervently held that the only way to prevent the
children from being caught in the cross-fire was to divide their
care equally between us. And, in order finally to draw a legal line
under our collective misery, I also insisted on a divorce.

Thus we became two 'one-parent' families who spent large
chunks of time travelling between Brighton and London so that the
children could enjoy their weekends and holidays together. I found
work that would allow me to pick up my son from school; or, when
he was older and able to walk home by himself, that would never
keep me in the office past five o'clock. Friends and family rallied
round. As did a variety of girlfriends, for I hadn't allowed the fact
of my divorce, or my internal confusion, to stop me acting as
heterosexually as possible.

Of course, I still fancied men, and had lately – when my son
was staying with his mother – begun to experiment more and
more widely with any number of gay possibilities. Pubs, clubs,
Soho cinemas, outdoor cruising, cottaging: all started to figure in
my life. Yet I still believed that only with a woman could I hope
for any degree of emotional stability or commitment. Until, in
1984, I met a man (I thought purely for sex) who, at a stroke, made

me realize the full extent of my self-delusion. For the first time ever, I tumbled hopelessly, gloriously into that state of tortured suspension we call 'being in love' – and not even the fact that my quarry wasn't remotely interested in reciprocating my passion could detract from how ultimately happy this made me feel. After many years – a lifetime – I was at last comfortable in my own skin. Fully out of the closet. Standing in the light. Liberated. Complete.

That the man I'd fallen for was not called Peter is by the by: he comprehensively paved the way for Peter in that when, soon afterwards, Peter and I met, I was more than primed. But of course there were problems. My son was just 13. How the hell to introduce a strange man into our lives? The simple answer was: I couldn't, except perhaps by stealth. So we pretended merely to be friends, never sharing a bed unless my son was away, until the fateful day when Irene, scenting what was afoot in spite of our caution, issued me with a lawyer's letter. As a practising homo-sexual, the letter chillingly informed me, I could no longer be considered a fit parent and my ex-wife was therefore taking me to court to seek custody of our son.

As with our split-up and subsequent divorce, what followed was distressing in the extreme. Mistrust, anger, thwarted love, bewilderment, spite, opportunism, God, the lack of God: all played their part, venomously on occasion. But the main thing for me was, and remains, my instinctive decision not to deny a rela-tionship with Peter. I didn't for one instant relish exposing my young son to my sexuality; but to have pretended that I felt other than I did about Peter would, I resolved, have entailed a degree of dishonesty that even I, despite a lifetime's practice, could suddenly not have endured.

And so I fought the case, again with the considerable help of family and friends, and went on to win it, too, thanks to the most skilful of solicitors and our great good luck, when the case did eventually come to court, of landing a sympathetic judge.

At which point, we were dealt a further surprise. My son announced that he would henceforth prefer to live with his mother. As he later explained, he felt that he and I had enjoyed enough of a 'run' together; now it was his mother's turn. Though of course, what he might actually have been saying was that the court case, and all that it entailed, had simply been too difficult for him to handle. As, indeed, it had for all of us, in different ways.

So does my ending qualify as happy or unhappy? Miraculously, albeit with reservations – maybe, atheist that I am, I must nevertheless grant that there is a God who sometimes moves in mysterious ways his wonders to perform – by and large it qualifies as happy. After my son had left, there was no longer any reason for Peter and myself not to move in together, or to become what we have since very contentedly become: a domestic partnership that has spanned some 20 years. Irene, too, has found happiness with Keith, both our children with their respective spouses, and although there are still (and perhaps always will be) no-go areas in the story of our family, when we gather together to greet the arrival of new grandchildren, currently totalling four, the occasions are joyful, even when Peter jokingly complains that grandfatherhood by proxy is not what he, as a gay man, had envisaged for his old age.

Added to which, he and I can now also contemplate legalizing our own union, while in South Africa there exists a new constitution that grants to gays and lesbians a degree of rights and respect that would, in my youth, have been unthinkable. Were I to be starting my journey afresh, how much easier it would be, how much smoother!

Or would it? Because when all is said and done, I happen to

believe that uncertainty is intrinsic to the human condition. My not knowing myself was what, in the end, provided me with the answer; made me live the way I do now. As the proverb has it: the longest way round is the shortest way home. And besides, the many difficulties of my journey notwithstanding, I have still been lucky enough both to have my cake and to eat it. Delicious it is, too, fairy cake – so delicious, so suffused with unexpected tastes and textures that I am even tempted, and sometimes able, to write about it. Not as Shakespeare would; but then you can't have everything, even as queen of your own bed.

Stella Duffy

We live in a house, a London terrace, small front garden, two receptions, three bedrooms, back garden. We do not live in an especially salubrious part of London, we pretty much swapped a one-bedroom flat in north London for this three-bedroom house in south London. We chose inside space and garden over location. This year the cherries and apples and tomatoes and single pear in our tiny town garden proved it was the right choice. The harvest from the two bedrooms-that-are-offices are equally prolific – we write plays, radio, novels, articles, ideas. This is a typical London terrace. And I have no idea what that typical means now.

My mother was born in a terrace just like this, a mile or so away in Kennington, in 1921. The house she lived in was shared – her aunt, uncle and cousins in one half, she and her parents and two brothers in the other. My wife Shelley and I share our house with a cat. We'd hoped to share it with children; we tried, they didn't happen. We have been together for 15 years, and in that time have lived through parental rejection, parental acceptance, three house moves, cancer, miscarriage, failed IVF, infertility, parental death, the births, deaths, weddings and divorces of friends and family, along with countless dinners and lunches and parties and barbecues and nights in with dinner on our laps and rubbish telly to be laughed at and not enough holidays and too many deadlines.

We've had three weddings. The first, a very small one when I was still exhausted from cancer treatments, was a celebration of ten years together and getting through the cancer year. It was at home, with our best friends, intensely private, and very emotional. The second was our Partnership Registration at City Hall, on a late summer day, with a view of Tower Bridge, in front of

30-odd family and friends, followed by a repetition of vows and party for 180. The third at 9.30 a.m. at the Lambeth Registry Office on 23 December 2005, our Civil Partnership, granting us the legal and pension rights long enjoyed by heterosexual married couples (many of whom are often so blithely unaware of the privileges they possess). To me, the most important right, as a woman who has (touch wood, so far) made it through a life-threatening illness, being that of next-of-kin. As my civil partner, Shelley can, if necessary, make medical decisions for me. Further, having registered my own mother's death, I know what an important thing that is to do for someone, to honour their life in the same way a birth is honoured, recorded, witnessed. We live in a witness culture. Since our Civil Partnership, my partner now has the right to honour – bear witness to – my life in this way, and I hers. It is a long overdue right, but nonetheless welcome for that.

When I was coming out in the late 1970s and early 1980s I was terrified, of my difference, and divergence, of being alone. Born in London, I grew up in a small mill town in New Zealand, the youngest of seven children in a working-class family. For such a family there, then, we were well read. But Orwell and Huxley, Austen and Brontë are hardly an introduction to gay life. At 15 I hadn't yet read the novels – many of which were still to be written – that might suggest being 'different' could also be special, be good. I didn't know any lesbians, I didn't know that what I was feeling had anything to do with being a lesbian. The one lesbian role I knew was Sister George, and I'd only seen that on TV because my father thought Beryl Reid was the funniest woman alive. The ensuing film wasn't exactly what he had in mind. Nor did it, with its classic doomed lesbian relationship, offer any hint of what my life would be. Not only that, but much as I was starting to consider working as an actor, I didn't fancy being Susannah York, or Beryl Reid or even Coral Brown. I didn't fancy any of them either. (Well, maybe Coral Brown, just a little.) There were no lesbians on television, in the movies, in my books, in my life. Or so I thought. Years later I was to find that my uncle's sister had had a 'friend' all her adult life, that when the mother of the boy up the road moved out from their family home, she moved in with another woman. But these were secrets, hidden. These women were not able to be role models for me not merely because they weren't out, but because everyone else refused to be out about them as well. They were there, and they were invisible.

Of course, at the time, there were very few women – as heroes, at centre-stage – anyway, so of course the chances that any of them would be gay women were commensurately lower. And yes, we have done better and times have changed and 30 years have made an enormous difference. We've come a long way babies. But . . . in terms of media visibility, of role models for young girls (or even old women), there is still a very long way to go. Where gay men had *Queer as Folk* in the 1990s, lesbians had the grumpy boring dykes in *Queer as Folk*. Where gay men had John Hannah and Simon Callow's happy (if doomed!) couple in *Four Weddings and a Funeral* at the movies, we had Sharon Stone portraying a homicidal bi-bitch. How many out gay men in parliament, how few out lesbian. Yes, there is *The L-Word*. On cable. Not even Channel 4 was brave enough to go there.

We're simply not there yet, and feminism – as much as 'gay liberation' – still has a role to play in getting lesbians into the mainstream. With approximately 75 per cent (at a conservative estimate) of British TV companies, theatres, film companies, newspapers, TV channels, film distributors, publishing houses, magazines owned and / or run by men (and not all of them straight men by any means) we're a long way from lesbians owning or running the means of production whereby we might see ourselves reflected back. No wonder we so rarely see representations of ourselves we recognize, in our many forms, in our multiplicity. Nor do I believe this is all the fault of the men in charge, not entirely. The men running our media and government are there because they've always been there. Because it's what we all – men, women, gay, straight, black, white, brown – are used to. Not all that long ago the Brontë sisters had to sell their work under men's names. Change takes time. We're doing better than we used to. Way better than seemed possible to this small-town girl in 1978 – but not quite well enough.

One of the reasons this change is too slow is that not everyone is engaged in it. Not all the lesbians are engaged in it. I know several lesbians who work in the City and say it's impossible for them to come out. Really? Harder than for the Muslim and Jewish and Christian and Sikh lesbians who are out to their religious families? I know so many women who say they can't tell their parents because they are too old or too sick or too religious or simply won't understand. Well no, not without it being explained to them they won't. I know way more out gay men than out lesbians. I suspect most of us do, whatever our sexual orientation. And yes, I do work in a 'nice' media world where (usually) people are fine about my being a dyke – but not always, not every time. And I don't actually live in that world. I live in a south London terrace, between an elderly Irish couple and a bunch of French students. Our GP knows we're together. Our dry cleaner knows we're a couple – over the years he has become a friend, we talk about the weather and the world and religion. A Muslim, he's asked me how Shelley and I reconcile our 'lifestyle' with our family faiths of Judaism and Catholicism. My answer is that it is no more a lifestyle than the colour of my hair or the freckles on my skin – my sexuality is both intrinsic and incidental to my life, but it is no choice. The guy at the petrol station where we buy petrol and crisps and drinks for long journeys asked if we were sisters. I said no, partners. When we bought our wedding dresses – together – (not meringues) and the sales assistant asked what was the occasion, we looked at each other, took a breath, told him. When the young and not-entirely-sober scaffolder, sitting beside me on the train to York last year, asked what I do and where I was going, he eventually got around – as I knew he would – to asking didn't my husband mind me going away for work so much. I explained that I was wearing a wedding ring as the wife of a wife. He then asked didn't she mind me going away for work so much. Confounding both my expectations and those of everyone else sitting near us who had suddenly become ever so interested in their fingernails as they stopped talking themselves and listened for his response.

Yes, it is boring coming out all the time. The tedious predictability of the double take, of being – at best, at least – interesting. I'm 42, it is a very long time since I thought being 'interesting' was a career option. Coming out always feels a little more intrusive, like giving a little more information than is asked for. But then again, people will chat at bus stops and in supermarket queues, they will ask about work and partners and children. And I will tell the truth. Every single time there is a moment of tension, an uncertainty, and not every reaction is OK by any means, but my black and Asian friends have no choice about being out as their 'minority' – we do. My choice is to be honest. I believe change will happen faster that way. I believe I have a duty to make change faster and being out easier for the next lot of 14-year-old girls looking for the lesbians in their world. Where are the lesbian pop stars and movie stars and soap stars, the lesbian business leaders, the lesbian entrepreneurs, the lesbian religious leaders? They're not out. They're letting the rest of us make the world safer and easier and better for them, while they lie. And I'm tired of it. I want them doing the work too. If everyone who has ever had a homosexual love, desire or experience came out right now, the world would change overnight. We could stop being interesting or different or special because we're gay, and get on with just being.

Meanwhile I live in south London. I live with my wife. My family speak of her as their sister-in-law. I go to Friday night dinner at my in-laws. Both my parents are dead, my in-laws see me as theirs now. None of this has been easily won, none of it was handed to us on a plate, none of it came without a struggle. We pushed for nine-and-a-half years to be accepted as a couple in our families. There were six teenagers at our big wedding party, young people who may or may not find they are gay as time progresses, young people who saw that their parents and families both valued and validated our relationship. For me, the most important part of these (necessarily) self-made ceremonies was that we were witnessed. Before the Church took over marriage, and priests became involved, partnerships were always formalized in front of one's community, whether that involved jumping over a broom or literally tying a knot. I have learned that the public declaration of love is remarkably similar to the public declaration of sexuality. Of course it is easier to be out in a couple than as a single person. Most things are easier with the support of a partner. It is easier for the world – which likes things in pairs – to accept us as a two. But I'm not always with my wife, and my work very often takes me away from home, and when I am working or travelling alone the questions that prompt me to come out now are easily as frequent as they ever were when I was single. I look forward to the day when my wedding ring does not automatically imply that I have a husband.

With each small and personal and sometimes very hard and sometimes very simple declaration of truth we are honest on our own behalf and also, hopefully, make things easier for those young lesbians and gay men coming after us. Just as the lesbians and gay men before us made enormous and brave and sometimes small and often scared changes in their turn. Making it possible for us to be legally out. Making it possible for us to be Civil Partners. Making it possible for us to have tried to become parents. I know that as a lesbian in my forties I am enormously indebted to the women and men, both gay and straight, who came before and won for us the freedoms and rights that we – in the West at least – so often take for granted. I'm lucky, I have an interesting job, I like having an interesting job. In the rest of my life though, I'd be very happy to leave behind the double take. We are getting there. We're not there yet. We need many more of us in the process. Come on out, the water's fine.

Craig Jones

In 1993 a former Royal Air Force Officer named Robert Ely set up Rank Outsiders to support and seek justice for members of the Armed Forces dismissed for being gay. In a case which made legal history, and with the style that the service would have expected from its brightest and best, the Rank Outsiders pursued the Ministry of Defence (MOD) through every court that would hear their case until finally the European Court of Human Rights found in their favour on 27 September 1999. Gay servicemen and women of my generation will always be indebted to the Rank Outsiders for their determined pursuit of equality and justice, which gave so many others and me the chance to take our place.

On 12 January 2000, the Secretary of State for Defence announced the new policy to a packed House of Commons in terms which reflected the troubled path through which the changes had been achieved: 'There will be those who would have preferred to continue to exclude homosexuals but the law is the law. We cannot pick and choose the decisions we implement.' And so this policy was 'Hobson's choice', born in a storm and implemented through legal obligation. The change followed ten years of rhetoric-fuelled argument which had absorbed page upon page of national newsprint, mostly reporting the concerns of some of the Services' most senior commanders. In the years that immediately followed, the new approach was handled by civil servants in a manner which reflected this acute sensitivity to change.

My Commanding Officer announced the policy to a packed Officers' Mess. My response was swift and instinctive; I stepped from my closet and claimed the ground for which Rank Outsiders had fought so hard.

The House of Commons announcement freed me from the wearying necessity to guard the detail of my life for fear of repercussion. Secrecy and deceit go against the grain of the often-enduring friendships that we enjoy in the armed forces; practices that had caused many to feel a necessity to quietly depart the service for a more honest and less complex life. The right to privacy is important. However, in practice servicemen and women know a great deal about the lives of our colleagues because we choose to be open. The early months of 2000 were tough. My ship's company seemed to recognize that my choice of openness set me on a difficult path and I felt their growing support. I cannot immediately think of a civilian life equivalent to the support afforded by the 'band of brothers' that exists in the wardroom of a warship. It was profoundly rewarding to see attitudes and ideas about being gay change over time, but without audible corporate support for the new policy, I found the experience somewhat intense.

In May 2001, when I walked through the door of the MOD as the Vice-Chair of the newly formed Armed Forces Lesbian and Gay Association, there was not a champagne cork or rose-petal thrower in sight. There were, however, a handful of civil servants and their uniformed equivalents, with no agenda, no actions, no initiatives and ideally no homosexuals – but 'the law is the law'! Their trench was dug, so I left the building and looked for progress elsewhere.

In 2002 a MOD review of the impact of the policy noted that there were no problems to report – hardly surprising, with only a handful of people who had felt able to leave their closets and none of those consulted by the study group to ascertain their experiences. I suspect the author of the review was relieved to place the file in the back of the drawer:

Strength of activity is assessed as low – no gays detected.

In the early days of my growing involvement in Diversity and Equality, I found that corporate support was a decidedly hit-and-miss affair and I often envied standard-bearers from female and ethnic minority groups who much more readily attracted the support of key officers for their ground-breaking efforts. Despite the prevalence of tabloid press statements about 'political correctness gone mad' the reality is that the wider society vogue that suggests 'gay is good' had not then found a foothold with the policy-makers who guide our military lives. Many senior officers might admit to having been shy of the risk they associated with initiatives to support our gay men and women. The ice has thawed, but in earlier times it felt like sitting on an iceberg watching for signs of global warming. I got frostbite before being drowned in the warmth of acceptance.

As an initially unsupported 'voice' I felt that the only way to cause a ripple was through the media. There can be no doubt that the press can be the greatest catalyst of rapid change, and even bad press can keep the pot boiling. It was a tricky start! Without the benefit of access to a press officer I embarked upon a comedy of arrangements with a variety of hacks from the press pack. Some were like-minded terriers who were keen to take forward a novel story; others were sniping wolves who were searching out satire for the Sunday papers. I have learned that my gaydar is far from perfect when dealing with journalists. These involvements were only permitted after civil servants in Whitehall had checked and rechecked the pages of Queen's Regulations looking for a let-out – but none existed. More by luck than judgement, *Gay Times* undertook the first piece (gaydar not required!). It was a simple, but well-written human interest story and its final line propelled the reader to the front line, indicating that I was currently with a multinational task force in the Aegean and was pleased that my partner would soon fly out with 'the wives' when the ship was in a Turkish port. Two days after landing on the top shelf of news-stands, the story bounced across to the front page of the *Sunday Times*. Four days later the Turkish press arrived 'mob handed' on the gangway of another ship in our task force, demanding an interview with the operations officer or his boyfriend. Thankfully my friend and colleague on HMS *Suffolk* was married and had a sense of humour. A day later the Turkish headlines read: 'NAVAL OFFICER AND BOYFRIEND TAKE HONEYMOON IN TURKEY'. Had this been true, I could have claimed to be the last queen to be transported on honeymoon by a ship flying a white ensign – but in those stern times I fear the pun may have fallen flat.

In the early years I became accustomed to collecting my Sunday paper with a degree of trepidation – the perils of associa-tion with the media should be learned at university and not while digesting your Sunday cornflakes. Today the MOD and the services routinely place articles in the gay press and I have access to a wonderfully supportive press officer who does her level best to keep me on the right side of Queen's Regulations, fending off the wolves with their 'Hello Sailor' headlines and allowing me a little leeway from the corporate line. I know from my mailbag that articles illustrating the experiences of junior sailors, soldiers or airmen and junior officers have a hugely positive impact upon serving readers and potential recruits.

Media coverage is nevertheless only a small part of the process by which the armed forces have started to desensitize this issue and achieve change. Not long after the lifting of the ban, I was confronted by an officer who felt I was overstating my concerns about the underlying attitudes of senior commanders, adding that his wife knew some gay people and they had even been to supper! In response I challenged him to purchase a copy of *Gay Times* from his newsagents over the coming weekend. He called me on the Monday morning to say that he had stalked the magazine rack for a good half-hour but not found the right moment. His effort and his honesty won my loyalty. Far too often those who struggle with these issues are neither earnest nor willing to discuss. Increasingly, our senior managers accept the need for strong leadership and corporate moral courage, not shrinking violets, but in 2000 there were no policy implementation plans, no associated initiatives, no lectures, no roadshows, and no external or internal public relations efforts. I am quite convinced this had nothing to do with homophobia; it was simply a policy that nobody wanted to be seen to develop or champion. There could have been no more profound herald of the end of this period than Vice-Admiral Sir James Burnell-Nugent's support for the Royal Navy's membership of Stonewall's Diversity Champions programme in February 2005. This is in stark contrast to the two years that followed the lifting of the ban, when senior officers from all three services had nothing to say about their gay men and women, excepting a comment to the *Western Morning News*, again by Vice-Admiral Burnell-Nugent, suggesting that the matter had been less challenging than bringing women to sea. Joining the Stonewall Diversity Champions programme has been a watershed for the Royal Navy and I hope that the Royal Air Force and the Army join the 150 or so corporate members in the not-too-distant future. No doubt there are still some admirals, air marshals and generals who are not yet convinced that such bold initiatives are necessary; however, I know that those who work with our more junior servicemen and women recognize the value of our growing confidence as an employer of gay men and women.

Over the last five years I have observed that officers who are routinely lucid and forthright in the execution of their duties seem to have 'first day at school' meekness when dealing with the word 'gay'. Not so long ago I sent an e-mail to our Diversity Team advising that many of my gay colleagues bemoaned the fact that despite being 'out' at work, their senior officers had never found a mechanism to acknowledge their orientation, such as ordinary bar chat about home life. Because the e-mail was transmitted outside my chain of command I sent a courtesy copy to my then Commanding Officer, whom I held in particularly high regard. Not more than two hours later he plonked himself in an adjacent chair in the Mess and asked after my plans for the weekend. I accept readily that many people simply do not know how to react. Ignorance is not a constant state for most and we have all been guilty on some occasions of actions that were not well founded in fact or knowledge. Achieving change requires a willingness to be informed and a willingness to impart. I feel assured that the former quality exists in the vast majority of our men and women, and increasingly our gay men and women feel able to play a role towards achieving the latter. The fact that I am still the most senior gay officer in the vanguard of this initiative tells me that there is still work to be done.

While my actions and beliefs have always been those of a champion of equality, for some time I was seen more commonly as a challenging protagonist of gay rights. Looking back, I'm quite sure that this was unavoidable. I reluctantly accept that change takes time and I am grateful that the many senior officers who have received a letter, e-mail or, far worse, an appearance from me over the years have taken my direct style with a pinch of sea salt and listened to what I had to say. It is sometimes difficult to tell the difference between those who have insight and those who are simply incensed; on most occasions I feel I had a little of both, but would add that our practice today largely reflects my first writing on the subject from 2000.

Are the armed forces institutionally homophobic? I would be ill at ease with such a conclusion, which would do a great disservice to an overwhelming majority of our men and women. At an individual level, most have taken the changes since 2000 within their stride, helping our gay men and women find their place in each ship, regiment and squadron. For reasons I have made clear, our more junior members have often led the way with their more recent experiences of sanguine attitudes commonly found in civilian life. I chatted to a gay soldier some months ago about his experiences of being at the front line during the 2003 Iraq War. With a cheeky grin he lamented that his fellow infantrymen seemed 'far more interested in invading Iraq than me and my sexual orientation'. There are elements of the extreme in all walks of life; however, I believe that our approach to these issues has been tinged with nothing worse than the conservatism of middle England. Many senior managers are respectfully shy of tricky personal issues or matters, especially where the relationship between risk and reward is ill defined. In reflection of this, our efforts to make our gay men and women feel welcome were initially inadequate. Increasing awareness by senior officers of the benefits of being a demonstrably good employer of gay men and women will set the foundations of our enlightened approach in the forthcoming years.

Most major employers have acknowledged the benefits of ensuring that diversity and equality teams include gay personnel. The armed forces is one of the UK's largest employers, with tens of thousands of people living and working in challenging circumstances across the globe, day in, day out. There was an obvious necessity for a supporting education programme, led by gay personnel. In the early years of the new policy I dealt with many sailors, soldiers and airmen whose experience of 'coming out' in their unit had been traumatic, leaving them at best bewildered and in some cases unable to cope. Some cases involved considerable hardship. I am relieved that these cases have become far less common in recent years and the services are increasingly adept at providing support where it is needed.

Looking ahead, and astern, through my telescope, I see the armed forces making significant progress but at noticeably different paces. In 2005 the Royal Navy joined Stonewall's Diversity Champions programme, attended Brighton Pride and convened its first Conference for Gay Personnel. I am no longer alone in recognizing that it will take a greater effort if we are to melt away the impact of the armed forces' 20-year 'gay ice-age'. Our Diversity and Equality staff and key gay officers and ratings have worked together at the vanguard; however, the arrangement seems ad-hoc given the special circumstances in which our people live and work, and none of the services employ gay officers' in their Diversity and Equality teams. I concede that the pace of change and style of initiatives demanded have almost always seemed a step too far to many. My northern heritage has always guided me to ask for more than I might reasonably expect to get!

Gay men and women are now serving with distinction alongside their heterosexual colleagues, with increasing levels of support from their commands and service chiefs. We no longer dismiss highly trained and much-needed personnel. It is now unequivocally accepted that the armed forces cannot afford to make moral judgements about the sexual orientation of men and women who serve with loyalty and dedication.

The armed forces is one of the UK's largest employers and therefore we could possibly be one of the UK's largest employers of gay men and women. I hope that in the coming years we continue our progress towards achieving the type of changes that will ensure that our gay men and women are universally welcomed for who they are, valued for their contribution and respected for their willingness to take their place in the communities of the armed forces. If we genuinely aspire to be a world-class employer of gay men and women, there must be no let-up in our efforts to achieve genuine change – indeed, they must gather greater pace.

Irshad Manji

*Would it be fair to say that in every aspect of life you inhabit a kind of
exiled or outsider position? Not only your sexuality, of course, but also
being expelled from Uganda as a child and becoming a refugee in
Canada. Furthermore, there is your attitude towards your faith and
religion.*

I think it would be more than fair to say that. A lot of that is happily
so. When you're on the outside but still working within the param-
eters of an overall public you actually have a very liberating
vantage point. Because you see you have already disappointed so
many people by virtue of being who you are and insisting on being
who you are it frees you to follow your own vision and not worry
about betrayal since you've already betrayed. So there are those,
for example, who would want to call me a sell-out – whether from
the gay and lesbian community because I'm not as strident as
many of them are about particular issues; or the Muslim community for obvious reasons; or the feminist community for believing
that religion and women's equality are not necessarily incompatible. For all of those reasons, the best and most truthful answer is, I
never bought in to your norms and I've always believed that to be
queer is first and foremost to be unconventional. And that frankly
doesn't have to depend on your sexual orientation. I remember
when I was presenting and producing *Queer Television* in Toronto,
which was at the time the world's first programme on commercial
TV to explore the lives of gay and lesbian people, the most vitriolic
hate-mail that I received in season one came not from Christian
fundamentalists, nor from Muslim literalists, but from gay and
lesbian militants.

They accused me of betraying the cause. Because I conceived of

Queer Television as being a programme that is honest about the world – and that means having to take into account the reality checks of our world, including homophobia that exists. So I would air anti-gay comments as much as pro-gay comments on the show and I would encourage our viewers to respond with counter-argument rather than with slogans about victimhood. And my gay and lesbian critics argued that diversity of appearance was all that really mattered.

My argument was that diversity of expression also matters if we're going to take democracy – the very democracy from which we benefit – seriously. I think that moment crystallized for me the virtue of reaching out across borders and ensuring that straight people can relate to the show because you're being honest and authentic, not because you're preaching; that grandmothers can relate, teenagers, immigrants, the curious, and even the bigots. It's all about, as I said, being unpredictable. I realized that not everybody accepts this definition of queer. They don't have to. It is mine, and I stand by it.

Was it your intention to become mainstream?
Not for the sake of being mainstream, no. But certainly one of the purposes of reaching out beyond easy boundaries is to help people appreciate that the struggle for diversity and conformity is a very elemental, even eternal struggle. And it's a human struggle. I'm not the kind of person who likes airy-fairy rhetoric about common ground and about taking unity from diversity and what we all have in common is more important than our differences – often it's not more important. Often people do seek out ways of being special, and unique and precious, because that is the source of their identity. But I just think it is far more interesting, much more fascinating, to explore what is unpredictable about all of us, rather than what is rigid and absolute, and frankly

dull. So for that reason I wanted to break down walls, and in the course of doing that we reached the kind of audience that allowed us to win Canada's highest broadcasting award for – get this – Best General Information Programme. Some would say, that's mainstreaming – oh, ok, if that's mainstreaming then so be it, but I'm much more interested in being relevant rather than main-stream, and I think that is the key distinction.

You've written about sexuality as one among many gifts of God. Do you recall when you first realized you were gay?
Yes I do. I was a legislative assistant to a Member of Parliament in Canada, working on Parliament Hill, and befriended someone who came out to me as being a lesbian, and I remember looking at her and thinking to myself, 'You're not ugly – how can you be a lesbian, you're not ugly', and it might sound shocking how somebody who now advocates universal human rights on a global level can possibly be so simple-minded. Well the truth is that even in the progressive political circles in which I operated, I never came across an out lesbian. Out gay men, yes, but never an out lesbian. This would have been mid- to late 1980s – unbeliev-able, how can that be?

So I remember that over time we became closer and I realized I was falling in love with her. And I called my mother, to say that I'm coming home to explain to you why I am so happy. Over tea and toast one Sunday morning, I told my mother exactly what she knew she would be hearing. And the tears streamed down our faces, and she asked me all of the important questions, like 'Are you sure it wasn't your father's violence that did this to you?' And I said I know lots of straight women who have been abused by their fathers. 'Are you sure this isn't a phase?' I told her I actually don't know if this is a phase – it might be, all I can tell you is this is where I am right now. What I loved was after the conversation she said to me, 'Look, I love you as much now as I ever have. This doesn't change anything for me.' And I really appreciated those words – both for the obvious reason, because who wants to be disowned? But also because she didn't resort to histrionics – she didn't throw her arms up in the air and say 'Thank you for being so honest with me, I love you more now than I ever have.' And more than that, my mother pulled out my ninth-grade student ID card: I looked at it and I bristled. If ever there was a stereotypical lesbian, I saw her in that card. This was during the British invasion – Duran Duran, Culture Club: I had a short-cut, wearing safety pins, down to my knees, hanging from one of my ears, a cardigan – a very, very butchy look, and the funny and, I think, fascinating part of all of this is she predicted on the basis of a stereotype that I am what it turns out that I am.

How did you then reconcile the fact of your sexuality with your faith?
It wasn't an issue at first. On the one hand I had happiness, on the other hand I had religion. I knew which one I needed more. But then I began hosting *Queer Television* and received, in addition to mail from the gay and lesbian critics, hate-mail from people of strident faith who angrily challenged me to reconcile my homosexuality with Islam, saying 'You cannot be both Muslim and Gay.' And there were moments when in the course of having to respond, or feeling the need to respond to these angry challenges, I did also feel the need to excommunicate myself from Islam. Because an ultimatum was being placed in front of me, and I figured that must mean I had to make one choice or another. But every time I pushed myself to the brink of excommunication, I pulled myself back. Once again, it was out of fairness, out of fairness to myself. I had read the Koran for many years, and I knew that it contained many pro-diversity passages – passages, for example, that state that if God had willed he would have

created you all as one people, but he has done otherwise. Passages that say everything God makes is 'excellent', that nothing God has made is 'in vain', and that God creates 'whom he pleases'. Now all of these taken together made me ask the very basic question, if God had not wished to make me a lesbian, then why would he not have used his unparalleled, unmatched powers to make somebody else in my place? And that question has never been satisfactorily answered for me. So as long as the possibility, in my mind at least, exists, that my so-called deviation was intentional, and that I am indeed a creature of God, I have to believe that God knew what he was doing. Mind you, I am not for a minute suggesting that I am right and my critics are wrong. They may in fact be right; I actually accept the possibility that my creator may reject my same-sex relationship, how do I know? I don't know God's will – I will find out one day. I couldn't care less if Muslims accept homosexuality – I don't seek their approval. The only approval I seek is that of my creator and that of my conscience. And I already know that I've got that of my conscience; I'll find out later about my creator. The only thing I am asking Muslims to accept is that even in the Koran there is room for discussion on as thorny an issue as this.

What were attitudes to sexuality like in Canadian society when you were coming out?
Apart from the strident religious folk, I wouldn't say that it was a shrug of the shoulder for most people. It's hard for a lot of people I think these days to appreciate, given how far in less than a decade gays and lesbians in the West have come. It's hard for us to remember that there was a time prior to same-sex marriage/civil union legislation. Presenting and producing *Queer Television*, I wanted to make sure that there was very little sexuality in the programme for a very specific reason: I did not want to reduce

gays and lesbians to sex. There was and is so much more about us to explore. I think that approach mitigated a lot of fears that people had.

What motivated you to start the TV programme?
It wasn't my idea. The chief executive of the channel had been tracking my career for years. I had just finished writing my first book, about how young Canadians are redefining democracy in an age of fluid media networks and flexible personal identities and changing social balance. He said he had read the book, loved the message, and asked me to front a programme about gay and lesbian issues. My initial reaction was to refuse. But then he came back again and asked me what kind of programme I would like to do. I suggested broadening the programme to include issues that gay and lesbian people are at the centre of, but do it in a way that straight people can relate to, because that was about honesty and authenticity. My boss wasn't convinced, but we got the highest ratings of any of the programmes that were new to the channel, and that allowed my boss to make the argument that we now needed to be bumped up another level and not just be a local television programme, but also be internationally syndicated. So we managed to negotiate a syndication deal with Planetout.com which was at that time the world's biggest gay and lesbian web portal. It lasted three years. I left because I didn't want to be known just as that TV dyke – because I'm more than that.

There are dangers, aren't there, in imposing categories and solidifying identities?
Yes, what you wind up with are competing fundamentalisms. So, a gay man or a lesbian can say to a literalist Muslim, 'My fundamentalism is better than your fundamentalism.' But the reality is that fundamentalism reduces each of us – whether it is ideological,

whether it is religious, whether it is cultural, or even economic as in the case of neo-conservatism – to something less than our whole, multifaceted, often paradoxical, sometimes contradictory and therefore deliciously interesting selves. And that's why I happen to agree that absolutes are not necessarily true; they cannot be true because if you want to be authentic and you recognize that the world is not monolithic – that it is complex – then to harden it is to lie about it. And that is why absolutes cannot be truths.

Being a lesbian does not preclude you from being so much more. There are such things as capitalist lesbians. I happen to be one of them. What I mean is in the women's movement it is often still assumed that if you are a real lesbian, with credible politics, you are going to be a socialist. You're not going to be a capitalist. And this is an example of how you don't have to be exclusive in your identity in order to have legitimacy. I remember encountering a very passionate – God bless him – white gay man, for whom everything was about gay – *everything* – and he was very upset with me because I was juggling so many identities and he felt that I was not paying due deference to the gay identity. And I said to him, 'Because you're a man, and because you're white, and that is still in our society today considered part of the norm, of who holds power, as you perceive it the only thing that you have going for you in terms of making you special and unique and precious is that you're gay, and you are so invested in that one identity that you become a fundamentalist about it. Whereas the beauty of being many things at once is that you actually don't have to be steeped in it all of the time. And for that reason alone I don't think that I'm selling out – I'm being who I am. I'm not asking you to agree, but don't suggest to me that because it's all gay all the time for you, it must be all lesbo all the time for me. So to me it is so blindingly obvious that there really isn't a struggle to be both a lesbian and so much more.'

In your book you write of the promiscuity of values in the West . . .
Of course when I referred to that, I was putting it in the context of how many Muslims worry that a multicultural society will pollute the piety of their children because there are so many values from which to choose and, God forbid, literally and figuratively, that you should use values that will lead you down a path that is not straight. Funnily enough, Islam is known as 'the straight path' – it doesn't have anything to do with homosexuality as such, but I wanted to point out that double entendre. So, obviously, it does have to do with the promiscuity of values; but I worry about relativism, and in particular cultural relativism. I really do believe, unlike many people on the conventional Left, that anything should not go – in other words, we should have defined values in an open society by which most of us can live. I believe that the guiding value of a decent, open society is individuality. I mean the kind of individualism that says, 'I'm myself, and my society benefits from that uniqueness.' So there's a balance between the public good and personal rights. And I think that this is a value by which all kinds of people can peacefully live – people who consider themselves persons of faith, gays and lesbians and other free spirits. This is not rocket science by any stretch, but what cannot be abided according to the value of individuality are those who preach a kind of violent hate that imposes upon others a reluctance to be who you are. At that point you've broken the social contract based on individuality, and that's why in my perhaps new incarnation as a Muslim reformer, I am very critical of religious extremists, including Islamists, who have made this weird, really odious and unholy alliance with people on the supposedly progressive Left.

The reality, though, is that in London recently a gay man was murdered because he was gay. There are still these threats, there are problems. So what would a gay politics be now?
I want to answer with the best of intentions, but the truth is I don't care what a gay politics looks like. Why? Because I don't care about the category 'gay'. I care about the category 'queer'. And again, with the intent of explaining that it is about unconventionality (and this means for example in terms of politics and political movements), of not being afraid of asking questions out loud. In the immediate aftermath of 9/11, various Muslim civil rights organizations called on the public to pour into the streets and protest against Islamaphobia. And many did. I know of an openly gay politician in Toronto who attended those protests, and I later asked him, 'When you were at that protest, did you ask any of the Muslims around you if the next time a gay bookstore or a lesbian nightclub is firebombed, will they reciprocate with outrage – will they support your call to protest homophobia?' Of course he didn't ask them that. But why didn't he ask them that? 'I don't want to be perceived as a racist.' This fear of causing offence is very much a one-way street right now in the so-called progressive, including the gay and lesbian, movements. We are supposed to worry about not ruffling other people's feathers.

In the shift from 'gay' and 'lesbian' to 'queer', does it mean doing away with quite specific histories?
One can and, I think, should express gratitude for standing on the shoulders of people who have come before you, who have made it possible for you to be who you are in all your multiplicity. Let us never forget the struggles that continue to happen; but what I'm saying is that one can know of one's past, one can be grateful for one's past, without being governed by one's past. I think that that's an important distinction. There's a difference between

identity and integrity. Identities too often are formed by the need for social approval. 'It's what other people think of me', many of us subconsciously and sometimes consciously believe, 'that determines my identity.' If you truly believe that, then at a certain point you're going to ignore your own integrity and your own conscience. And I would any day choose being true to oneself over catering to other people's expectations. That means from time to time that one must choose integrity in order to have or reframe a new identity. That will be painful, that will be challenging, that will be difficult; but it's not impossible. And let me personally attest: it is very liberating. I'm not suggesting there has to be a contradiction between identity and integrity – not at all. When you define who you are and you reserve the right to change, to evolve, you are expressing your integrity, your wholeness. For me it's no contest – integrity wins out, because integrity allows me to decide what my identity is. I don't have to choose between the two: I just choose to get to where I want to be.

Sticking with this theme, you wrote about a need for 'proper representation' being dependent on shared values. How does this connect with queerness?

I was saying, 'Hang on a minute, why does "Proper Representation" of blacks depend on you having black skin? Why do gays and lesbians expect "Proper Representation" to come only from gays and lesbians, and similarly Muslims only from Muslims?' It seems to me that once again when you define that as Proper Representation you are reducing individuals to biological elements of their constitution. My point in challenging that was to say, 'How come we can't base proper representation on shared values? Like individuality? And why can't you as a white guy properly represent me? You have the capacity to.' And that's really what I'm getting at here. In the so-called progressive politics of today, too many of us are privileging our attachments – what we have, what we're born with, what we have come to expect of one another – over our capacities. And I'm all about capacity. I really believe that human beings have the potential to be so much more than tribal arrogance tells us we are. That tribal arrogance can come as much from gays and lesbians as it can from anyone else.

This struggle with tribalism and our own tribalisms is such a perpetual struggle, and I think it's necessarily a struggle because conformity is as much a part of human nature as the need to be different. When you're talking about movements such as the Gay and Lesbian Movement, and the Women's Movement, you see difference venerated to the point where you must conform to that difference, otherwise you're a sell-out, as that white gay man effectively told me.

There seem to be echoes of this queerness in your role as a Muslimrefusenik and your work on Project Ijtihad . . .
Project Ijtihad and my refusal to join an army of automatons in the name of any God – hence Muslimrefusenik – is all about independent thinking, and that is a huge concept. It's simple without being simplistic. Ijtihad was specific to Islam as a tradition. As a concept it is universal: the need to reconcile, for example, reason with faith, or the struggle to do so. We've seen in all the great religions of the world, dissidents who have tried, often at the expense of their own lives, to effect this kind of reconciliation. It's ambitious, but also it reflects the desire of many people to not have to choose between two artificial distinctions: on the one hand to be a person of faith, on the other a rational human being.

What is your criticism of Islam?
My criticism is that literalism is going mainstream worldwide. I mean the rigid reading to the letter of the law if you will, taking

what the Koran says as finality and as absolute, as opposed to what many moderate Jews and moderate Christians take their holy book to be: as parables, as guides, but not necessarily the outright and the omega of what is 'true' for our world. When I say literalism is going mainstream worldwide in Islam, I mean Muslims even in the West are routinely raised to believe that because the Koran comes after the Torah and the Bible historically and chronologically, it is the final and therefore perfect manifesto of God's will – not given to the ambiguities, inconsistencies, outright contradictions and, God forbid, human editing like all of those other religious books. Even moderate Muslims accept as an article of faith that the Koran is not like any other holy book – it is 'God 3.0' and none should come after. What has happened is that interpretation has become imprisoned, so that even the Indonesian Muslim as a moderate will tell you that the Koran is the final word of God – that's it, no question asked. In my own critique, what I'm actually saying is that Islam itself once had a glorious tradition of progressive plural-istic thinking, that questioned even the Koran – this is Ijtihad and we need to rediscover it. This is something endemic to Islam, and there is nothing that has gone in the faith today that cannot be cor-rected. I'm actually quite comfortable making these sweeping statements because there is evidence for it. Arab cultural imperial-ism has managed over the last several hundred years to paper over those particularities that were once very vibrant in Islam, and that today are still vibrant in rituals and in packaging, but not in core practice. And that diversity in core practice is something I would welcome having restored.

Some say you have not engaged directly with the gay/progressive Muslim community in various countries . . .
This goes back to the conformity that I was talking about earlier: fine, be gay, be lesbian, have your difference, but don't be *queer*.

Don't have a viewpoint that is different from the consensus that we have developed. Otherwise you are not for real. You're not one of us. To which I respond: you're right, I'm not one of you. I'm not claiming to represent them – this is the caricature that it is assumed I buy into. And this assumption that I represent them means also that I must be betraying them. But I never claimed to represent, nor would I claim to represent, because we don't have shared values. This is a problem of people asserting the idea that we ought to share the same values. Why ought we to? Because I'm lesbian and Muslim and you happen to be as well: so bloody what? Are we not more than that? Is it not possible that we think differently? And is it not possible to celebrate that we think differently?

Why were you uninvited from the First International Queer Muslim Conference in Toronto?
I know, I smiled when I thought of that. I had not received any information about it. I had received a *pro forma* invitation to speak at it, because after all 'You're that lesbian Muslim we all know about and you've got a book coming out, how exciting', and then when the news hit that this book is not going to toe the standard party line, the disinvitations and so many others began to come my way. Sadly, it's both complicated and very simplistic at the same time.

So what next?
I'm undertaking a documentary film about what there is to love within Islam. As a struggling Muslim, I know what there is to quarrel about, what there is to believe, what there is to absorb and therefore frankly what there is to refute. What I don't yet know – and judging from the kinds of e-mails I get from other struggling Muslims, what many others don't yet know – is what is there to

love. And if 1.2 billion people out there get it, this is their time to enlighten me. In the New Year, 2006, I'll be a Fellow at Yale University under the auspices of the International Security Studies Program. And my chief mandate is to write my next book.

Will there be some kind of response to your critics?
I think some of the ironies of some of the supposedly progressive responses to my book will be incorporated into the next one, but not necessarily in a straightforward kind of way. I think one of the big questions that I'm going to address is what I would call the great liberal dilemma of the early twenty-first century. How do multicultural societies produce pluralists: people who appreciate multiple perspectives and truths, without producing relativists? People who can't or won't call it when culture becomes culture. When abuses are happening in the name of culture and we stand back and say nothing because we fear the 'racist' label. I think that's a huge dilemma for many people in Europe, and increasingly for people in North America. And given the multiple identities of which we have spoken, I think that somebody like me is in a position to shed light in new ways on this issue.

You point out challenges, which in many ways are creative, but this seems to get up people's noses . . .
There are two related reasons. The first: I express myself with confidence. And when I don't know the answer to something, I'm happy to acknowledge that, and I acknowledge that with confidence; and I think that really does rub insecure people the wrong way: 'Who the hell is she? How dare she revel in these ambiguities when we're all seeking conviction and certainty and stability and self-awareness?' But I would argue that it is precisely from ambiguity that we can tease out self-awareness because that's where the questions are, and questions are a much more honest

entrée into human nature than answers. The second reason is what I would call victimology, in which so many of the people who resent me wallow, and I think – not to make this sound infantile; I hope it doesn't – in their core a lot of the people who resent me are envious that I feel so comfortable doing what I'm doing.

I think you do need a thick skin. And you do need the ability to be called all kinds of names and accused of all kinds of conspiracies and still persist in doing what you're doing. And a lot of these people know that if they were under the gun, literally and figuratively, the way that I am every day they wouldn't be able to stand up to it. 'So who the fuck is she to *still* be doing this?' And really there's something deep in this: I've experienced it all my life. Not just now. All my life. Again, way back to *Queer Television*, there was a complex either within the gay or lesbian constituency that can be summarized as why her and not me? 'Why does she have this show and I don't?' And I would address this on camera: I would say, 'Have you done something meritorious lately?' Being gay, being lesbian is not an achievement, it's what you do with who you are that merits whether you're going to fulfil the dreams that you have. So don't tell me (because I'm not going to buy it) that on the basis merely of being gay or lesbian you are entitled to x, y or z. No, you're gay, you're lesbian, she's straight, he's celibate, so what? That's a tough message to swallow.

Is that one of the challenges that some gays and lesbians face?
Well, I wish it was one of the challenges they did face. That they did confront. It's one of the challenges that minority rights movements have to come to terms with. And I think that by virtue of belonging to minority groups we do not cease to be individuals. We are individuals within those groups. You can be both, but I am finding that in this rush to an overarching identity, 'group think' easily stifles individuality – and individuality is the essence of queerness.

Matthew Parris

If you need to shout about being glad to be gay, you probably aren't. Now I no longer have to shout, I really am. I have lived across a watershed. When I was a young man we were not glad to be gay, though with Tom Robinson in the Fairfield Halls in Croydon we waved our arms and shouted and sang and told ourselves we were glad, we really, really were – weren't we? But being gay was a thorn in your side and we knew it. We thought it would stay like that for the rest of our lives.

Now it isn't. It just isn't. I almost wish it were – it would be a challenge, it would make me braver. But for me today, in my work today and in my life today, it would be a bigger problem to be a Zionist or a convinced Christian than to be gay.

Never in my wildest dreams when I was young did I think the world we lived in then would change for the better as completely or as fast as it has. I remember at Cambridge resolving to stay celibate because after graduating I hoped to join the Diplomatic Corps. I felt sure that in some way or another I would be watched at university.

When I did become a junior diplomat I heard the whispers about the shameful secret of colleagues rumoured to be gay – senior colleagues whose careers (for reasons never spelt out) hadn't quite fulfilled their promise and who had had to content themselves with inferior postings in unimportant embassies. Will this be my fate? I thought. When a handsome young Bulgarian diplomat made a pass at me in a car I went straight to the Foreign Office security staff to report the incident – terrified nonetheless that the very fact of having had a pass made at me might cause them to speculate why, to ask what it said about me. We were paranoid then.

Now there is no bar on openly gay candidates for Foreign Office posts. A friend in politics tells me about how ministers arranged for one of our ambassadors to take his mother instead of a wife to run the social side of the embassy abroad. All this was inconceivable to me 30 years ago.

When I began the hunt for parliamentary seats whose Conservative constituency association might select me as their candidate, the most I dared do (and it seemed brave at the time) was refuse to lie about my sexuality; and refuse to talk about it at all. But I let others assume I was straight – I even let people think I had a girlfriend – and on the evening I was selected as Tory candidate for West Derbyshire a girl I knew made a point of getting an urgent message through to the chairman, before the vote, regretting that she could not be there. She knew the implication and so did I. We both knew I needed that.

As an MP I never did lie about sex, and of course in time everyone realized. But I never dared volunteer the truth. Though it might have spelt political suicide, I wish now that I had. Later I envied Chris Smith's courage.

How sharp is my memory of those early-1980s party conferences when, as Parliamentary Vice President of the Conservative Group for Homosexual Equality, I would struggle to find a venue prepared to accept us for our annual fringe meeting. How well I remember writing out the notices – 'CGHE' because some members were embarrassed to see it spelt out – and wondering whether anyone would come. How well all of us who were there then recall the dingy basements of second-rate hotels where we would make speeches declaring (what we did not believe) that 'the Party is changing', then drink warm, bad wine, bolt a handful of crisps, and melt into the night.

But the party really was changing, if only we'd known it. Like logs in a swelling logjam, social change in Britain was being blocked by timid and visionless politicians, but the blockage could only postpone the inevitable, and make the rush more headlong when the logjam broke. Stonewall was being born; John Major was inviting Ian McKellen to come and talk to him; Chris Smith was waiting to jump; and that seemingly solid wall of prejudice was about to disintegrate.

Today it is no bar in any of the mainstream political parties to be gay; in some Tory circles it is almost an advantage. There have been times when it would have been hard to throw a brick in the Home Counties without hitting a gay Tory candidate canvassing for votes. I smiled during the 2005 General Election campaign when *The Times* asked me to cover two seats with gay Tory candidates, Hove and Arundel. One lost, one won. Neither found their sexuality a problem. When on the doorstep I asked householders whether their candidate's sexuality was an issue for them, they looked at me as if I were some sort of throwback to the Dark Ages. I was. But the Dark Ages were only yesterday.

I might have stayed in Parliament if I had known how fast things would change. I knew, though, by the time I left to join the media in 1988, that in television and radio things were already changing. How fast, I had little idea. One morning in 1989 my blood froze as, just before going on air with my Sunday morning political programme, we read on an inside page of the *News of the World* that I had 'confessed last night' to being gay. Only the third of these assertions was true but I thought it might be fatal. It caused not a ripple.

In the news and entertainment media the only residual trace of the homophobic attitudes which ruled our lives 30 years ago is a measure of laddishness in what you might call the boiler rooms. There is none on deck and none on the bridge. And even at the sweatier end of newspapers, radio and television – the desks and studios where the finished product is actually knocked into shape –

I have never encountered unpleasantness or intentional insult: only the occasional ill-judged joke, or overheard remark about others.

The speed with which workplace attitudes towards homosexuality have been transformed is partly associated (I believe) with the growing numbers and status of women in what were once male-dominated preserves. In my field, the news and entertainment media, there are women everywhere and at all levels. They civilize.

It would be more interesting, I know, to say that huge difficulties remain. It would sound cleverer and more perceptive to say that the acceptance I find almost everywhere I want to go, and from almost everybody whose acceptance matters to me, is superficial – that on a deeper level I sense undercurrents of prejudice and incomprehension, undeclared.

But I don't. It is true of course that nobody truly 'understands' another person's sexuality, and that much of the heterosexual world is still quite ignorant about same-sex love, lust and partnership. But so what? I don't require understanding or familiarity – just respect and equality; and these are almost routine in my trade.

It would be less cavalier, I know, to say that I myself and my own experience are not the point; that maybe it's easier for the likes of me in the work I do and the circles where I mix; but that whole swathes of Britain are another country and one I do not inhabit; and here, there are mountains still to climb. Well maybe there are. Probably there are. But let's not be patronizing. Each of us speaks with most authority when we speak from our own experience – describe our own piece of the social jigsaw. We might allow the oppressed to speak for themselves rather than imagine ourselves into lives we do not lead and experiences which are not our own.

My own experience today is tremendously positive. Never in my entire professional career in the media have I ever once felt that I was denied a job or opportunity because I was gay. Never have I encountered the least difficulty in working with a colleague on account of their attitudes towards sexuality – mine or anybody else's. In radio, television and print journalism these days, the cultural norm – which treats homosexuality positively – is not at risk from homophobia. It is homophobes whose careers are at risk from the cultural norm. In the world where I work and do most of my socializing, homophobia is seen as the problem of the person in question, not those with whom he or she works.

Homophobes are the outcasts now. They are at a professional disadvantage and they know it. It would be like being the sort of Neanderthal who cannot work with women as superiors or equals: it would be he, not the women, who would be the victim of unpleasant gossip, whispered hostility and mysterious blocks to promotion. It would be he who would be perceived as having the problem.

A few years ago I was a guest at a supper-party hosted by a colleague in print journalism. It was a relaxed, informal affair. Over the meal the conversation turned to Section 28, which by then everybody agreed was doomed. One of the other guests, a convinced Roman Catholic, explained his own position, which followed Catholic doctrine. He had to regard homosexuality as a sin in the eyes of God, he said: as an abhorrent and unnatural practice. He set out his views politely – even apologetically. There was nothing aggressive or personal in his tone. I replied with arguments of my own. I noticed my host and hostess falling silent. Eventually they changed the subject and the conversation moved on. I left around midnight, having enjoyed the evening and the argument.

Next morning my host telephoned. He wanted to apologize, he said. He and his wife were acutely embarrassed by the views their other guest had expressed. They had been mortified that I had been (as they saw it) insulted in this way. But I had not been remotely insulted. The opinions I had disputed had been offered not out of a desire to hurt my feelings but as an honest outline of this guest's interpretation of the demands of his faith. I have often enough joined dinner-party debates about (for instance) abortion, divorce or adultery which were a good deal more heated and potentially 'insulting' to individuals. But in the case of a discussion by media folk on homosexuality, it was as though my feelings and beliefs as a gay man were somehow sacrosanct: to be protected against all criticism or question. I felt more embarrassed by my host's protection than I had been by his guest's robust opinion.

People are perfectly entitled to believe that homosexuality is a sin. I think they're nuts, but that's beside the point. There are people who think eating pork is a sin, and I think they're nuts too. We gays are not an endangered species or a rare and delicate breed of butterfly. We can look after ourselves. The world owes us civility, not admiration. In fact I sometimes think we are due for a bit of catching-up by the rest of the world. Maybe because of residual guilt about the last few thousand years, and more recently HIV/AIDS, we are given the benefit of moral doubts we do not deserve.

If over morning coffee a straight colleague in his thirties, forties or fifties were to regale his workmates with tales of the girls, barely out of school, whose bums he had pinched in the nightclub the evening before; if he were to amuse his audience with stories of casual sex in lavatories or dark corners; if he were to describe the sort of philandering which lads on Club 18–30 holidays used to boast of . . . then wouldn't most people think the less of him? But gay men with tales of predatory or promiscuous behaviour are indulged by straight friends and colleagues in an 'Ooh you are awful' sort of way – as though we inhabited a different world with different sexual morals, where the rules about harassment, exploitation and human respect were somehow suspended. On television, Graham Norton or Julian Clary get away with humour and innuendo which, because it is gay, is considered to be smart and quite sophisticated. If they had been straight men and a little older they would be in danger of being bracketed with Bernard Manning.

Part of the reason for the special protective stockade which media opinion has thrown around gay men is undoubtedly HIV/AIDS. An incurable disease is a tragedy in anyone's book and deserving of anyone's sympathy. Terminal lung cancer is a tragedy; syphilis – in the age when that was incurable and fatal – was a tragedy. Muscular dystrophy is a tragedy. Multiple sclerosis is a tragedy. But HIV/AIDS has not been seen as just another awful medical condition: it has been seen as a kind of curse, yet touched in a strange way by something close to benediction. I am uncertain of all the reasons for this; but one of them was undoubtedly because (at first, and when I was young) those who had contracted HIV or AIDS had not known, and had had no way of knowing, that this might happen, or how, and therefore had no way of avoiding it.

But that was the last century. Now we do know. Were I (in the company of the sort of people I mix with now) to compare the tragedy of the modern gay man who catches HIV to the tragedy of the nineteenth-century womanizer who contracts syphilis, the reaction would be outrage. Why? Both deserve sympathy and support. But both may have contributed to their misfortune.

It is time we stopped thinking of ourselves as special. This, as it occurs, will be the final act of emancipation. If we who are gay are to be, as we ought to be, equals in our sexuality with heterosexuals, if we are to demand and get the same rights, the same respect, the same opportunities, then the day is coming when we shall have to shrug off the special protection and – this is never acknowledged but it's what some gay men expect – the *sympathy* which, as the century turned, many of us still thought our due.

It was then. It isn't now. Self-pity is the final closet, and others' sympathies our final chains.

Sarah Weir

Come to the edge.
We might fall.
Come to the edge.
It's too high!
Come to the edge.
And they came,
and we pushed,
And they flew.

I once heard someone recite this Christopher Logue poem, written in 1968 to honour the fiftieth anniversary of the death of the French poet Guillaume Apollinaire. Immediately I heard it, it felt hugely relevant to the journey I feel I have made in my life.

I have made a few leaps, and when you talk about these, often well after the event, they can seem very easy and very smooth, as if everything was planned that way. In fact, the important moments in my life have often seemed to be about facing fear. About going to the edge. About jumping off. About hopefully always flying, but never being entirely sure you will.

I didn't know what I wanted to do when I was at school. Careers advice there was almost non-existent; I don't remember any of it. I just knew I was desperate to get out of the door the minute I was 16. I wanted to be free of a constraining environment. I wanted to get on. My parents' aspiration was that we become equipped to get married and then look after husbands. I almost stepped on to that path for a while, but I eventually found my own.

There are some mysterious years on my CV called 'Travelling'. It wasn't actually a gap year. After leaving school at 16 I worked in a local hairdressers, did a six-week cookery course, then worked for one year as under-matron in a boys preparatory school, darning socks and washing sheets.

But I saved up, not only to buy my first car – an old-style Beetle and my pride and joy – but also to buy a Laker Airways ticket to America. While out there, I did everything from looking after children and selling orange juice to tourists, to teaching Scottish dancing in Baltimore.

It was in 1979, the heady year Margaret Thatcher got elected, that I first moved to the City of London. As an unqualified girl, it was almost impossible to get a proper job, so through a connection I got an interview for a position as part broker/part typist (I told them I couldn't type). I spent my time opening the post, making the tea and delivering messages to smoke-filled rooms as the phone system was not connected to offices. I was there for 15 years, moving up to my first good position after five when I was made associate director. It was 1984 and I was 25. I then went on to become a director and finally managing director.

Looking back, it was a tough environment. I was a young woman in a generally male world, and quite unprepared. I came up through the company from the bottom – no management courses, no training. My chairman didn't believe in that stuff. You just did it. I think my chairman sort of saw me as an honorary man.

The male environment did have an effect on how I worked and how I behaved. When I started there were 50 women at Lloyd's among 5,000 men. Many of the old brigade didn't want to see women even leaving the kitchen sink. I had to serve a long apprenticeship, much longer than the men. You got looked up and down, your looks and clothes commented on, and there were sniggers as you sat down to do business. Women were only thought to be entering Lloyd's as a new marriage market. I could never understand why the market had to close for ages at lunch. I always arrived back early which meant I got more done. But it was very difficult to find your own personality. I looked 25 going on 50.

At the time, I didn't really see my time in the City as anything particularly out of the ordinary. I certainly couldn't have got on without an enlightened boss who pushed the chairman for me to be promoted – he who never quite got over the fact that I was a woman. Looking back, I suppose it was fairly pioneering. It was all pretty sexist and it was quite a battle – which affected the way I was, for good or bad. It created a defensiveness in me, a body armour. I absolutely hated being stared at and commented on. After I left, people asked questions about whether I'd been sleeping with my chairman. People assumed I must have been to get to the top like that.

I wasn't out in the City as a lesbian. I met my partner 13 years ago, in my final year. I definitely wouldn't have wanted anyone to know. I was very secretive about my life, which is not a good way for a relationship and something I wasn't comfortable about at all. I felt too insecure to be open about it. But it made me question myself, my values: not being able to be myself. I had no idea who else was gay then, in terms of women. It was incredibly closeted then too for gay men, a real secret society, but the word 'lesbian' only ever crossed people's lips as a term of abuse or ridicule. But in a way, being outside was sometimes an advantage. It meant I never took anything for granted. The good things were that I learned how to absorb facts quickly and to judge people's reactions and know when to stop. I hope I learned too how to deal with men, in particular those who were playing to the gallery and showing off. Bravado is so often a cover for something else.

Then I made it to managing director. So that was it. The top. Nowhere else to go. And was that it? It was a moment of terrible anti-climax. It was where I had supposedly wanted to be. I was expecting to meet so many new high-powered people that I could learn from and have as role models, but it didn't seem to be like that. I still wasn't really feeling fulfilled. It was stressful but not really intellectually challenging or even that difficult. It was also an environment I had never really felt completely a part of and it started to bother me. Was this it for the rest of my life? How real was this? It wasn't something I could really discuss with friends as they just saw this success story.

Thankfully, a friend told me to think about 'using your brain' in the arts and suggested I look at some female leaders in the cultural sector. So I did. I studied for a History of Art BA at Birkbeck in the evenings while still running the company. It was all a test to myself to see how I could cope outside a world I knew. It was Birkbeck that started to change everything. For the first time, I had female role models. My two main lecturers were women. They showed me a new environment. I opened my mind and used my brain.

When I decided that I would just start again in the arts, it was quite scary. I felt that all my props had been taken away. Now I was just left with me – and what did that mean? Who was I? What it meant was a visit to a bank manager whose face went pretty pale when I explained that I was re-starting my life and that my current outgoings massively exceeded my incomings. And that I had a job earning 90 per cent less than before. And I asked him to support this while I got going again.

It also meant no more red sports car, just a No. 19 bus. No more champagne for lunch, but a cheese sandwich in the café. It also meant re-discovering the value of money. My new job was at the Purdy Hicks Gallery. I'd bought many paintings from them over the previous ten years. They asked me to join them and soon I was making tea and sticking stamps on envelopes. It was all a real freedom from responsibility, almost like being on holiday for a year. I appreciated every moment as I knew I'd be unlikely to have it again. I did my degree and worked three days a week. I did things I had never done before.

My first front-line job in the arts was as a fundraiser for the Royal Academy. I'd never done this before. My first major sponsorship deal was with Goldman Sachs and Torie Legge-Bourke. I never forgot the first excitement of combining my business background with a knowledge of art.

Moving to work in the arts was a transformation for me. I had been married for just over four years in my early years in the City and took my husband's name. When I left the City, in the space of one year I changed everything – my job, my name, my sexuality, several of my friends. A really new life began and I started to really become myself. Then one day a friend saw a job as joint chief executive of the Almeida Theatre. It was a theatre I had known and loved since I first saw a poster campaign for it when I was in the City in 1990. I had never run a theatre, but they took a chance on me. It was a definite stretch of the elastic, quite outside my comfort zone of knowledge.

And now I have a great job as Executive Director of Arts Council England, London. I have responsibility for 115 staff and a £160 million budget. Our clients range from the Royal Opera House and the National Theatre to community theatre projects in outer-London boroughs. We're enablers, we're brokers, we're advocates. Much of our work is about stretching out, making links, about taking things further, about reaching those who don't or won't come banging on our door.

My role is to try and ensure that everyone living in London has both the choice and opportunity to engage with the arts as they want to: whether to go to it, do it or be it. Many people feel completely outside the arts, for a wide variety of different reasons. It is our job to break down some of those barriers, whether real or perceived.

You might say that it is easy to be openly gay now – you work in the arts. Well yes, but there are many more gay men with a definite support system than there are gay women. I don't really know many gay women through my professional life, even today. Being at the Arts Council has had some positive consequences. A small number of people who have worked with me have felt able to come out for the first time as they have felt I have shown that you can do it and survive. I haven't made a song and dance about it: I've just done it and talked about my partner when asked.

There is still prejudice in many ways in Britain – not just homophobia, but racism and sexism too. I became a trustee of Stonewall in 2003 as I thought it was time to stand up and be counted, to play my part in helping obtain equal rights for others now but also for the next generation.

I'm still very aware of the real pioneers who came before me, who made it possible for me to have the sort of opportunities I've had. I think that being outside things in many ways – as a woman in the City, as a gay woman in wider society – has made me what I am. I think it means I take a different perspective.

I'm more aware of what 'outside' might mean or feel like. And there are many people who feel outside many different aspects of the world we inhabit. They have to cope with far greater difficulties than I could even dream of.

I've had many opportunities in my life. I've gone to the edge several times and jumped off – with no crash-landings yet. Who knows how many more edges there are ahead of me?

I hope that this different perspective, this outsideness, actually helps me to bring others along too. To bring them to the edge. To help them jump. To help them fly.

David Starkey

I was born in Kendal in January 1945. My parents were that rather odd combination of being working class and Quaker. I was born with a double clubfoot, where the feet point backwards rather than forwards. I was very lucky and it was corrected, thanks to the NHS, and to the remarkable advances in orthopaedic surgery during the war, which came about largely because of the kind of injuries that they had to operate on. But of course parents, particularly mothers, take that sort of thing with desperate seriousness. So I had the classic gay childhood. If you wanted a case study for Freudian analysis of being gay, I would be it. There was a rather distant father – a good, kind, sweet man, but I think in a kind of internal exile, a bit from the marriage, and certainly from his life.

What did he do?
He was a shop-floor turner, a metalworker. In those days, of course, men weren't supposed to get involved very much at all in the upbringing of their children, and in a sense he was a perfectly good father. In fact we became very close. My mother was a classic working-class woman who really was the boss. The money, the wage packet, was handed over to her. She was also a hugely dominant, forceful personality, much more intelligent than my father but far less sensitive than he was. He loved poetry, was seriously religious. She was fiercely over-possessive and vastly ambitious for me, living out the things that she hadn't been able to do through me. She had been bright enough to go on to college but her parents hadn't been able to afford it, so the immense push that I received in education was due to her and, thank God, I was able to benefit from it. Otherwise it would have

been a deeply miserable experience. But she was a Pygmalion – she wanted me to be exactly as she wanted me to be. And the result was that I had an idyllically happy childhood, bar going to school. Going to school was the most horrible trauma – well, it was a typical crying your eyes out on the first day. I was at a very sweet, very progressive state primary school, run by a wonderful headmistress, Elsie Clyburn, who became a very close personal friend too, and it was deeply, deeply trendy. It was so trendy I actually got a prize for environmental science in 1956.

But I was an only child, there was the desperately over-protective mother, a domineering individual, and, as they say, the rest is history. And, of course, the fact that I was physically damaged meant that I tended to be a bit withdrawn and bookish. I didn't play games – again, a classic case study.

In terms of your sexuality, what can you remember?
Well, looking back from the very earliest stages, I had this tremendous interest in classical history that wasn't motivated by the history of the Roman Empire, it was lots of handsome naked men. One of the things, I think, with my generation, was that unless you were at public school, there was no language with which to express such things. The only time I ever encountered homosexuality actually discussed in my childhood was during one of those awful gay scandals in the local town, in which sweet innocent people – a vicar, a banker, somebody else, you know, totally consensual, totally among adults, all buttoned up – became the object of comment. That was monstrous, absolutely monstrous. But that was the only time that you ever encountered it. At school – an all-boys grammar school – it was very strange. There were all these funny games of grabbing balls, you know the standard thing. And looking back you can see that all the boys who went on and became gay didn't take part while all the straight lads did –

shocking behaviour in the rugger scrum and all the rest of it. Just typical male arsing around. I think the word 'homosexual' was first flung at me when I was a sixth-former and began to dandy. I wasn't really sure what it meant. Cambridge was very odd. There was just one couple who were sort of out, which was very unusual.

This was the mid-1960s, during my undergraduate years, which was just before everything happened. And there was what I can now see as an attempt at seduction. Over a bottle of disgusting sweet wine, which I've never been able to drink since, and my memory of it was a kind of bewildered horror . . .

Was that a sexual experience?
No it wasn't sexual at all, but you realize that something was going on. Eric, the person involved, became a friend, but I never found him attractive. And I was deeply unattractive at that point, being fat and pasty. I underwent this kind of transformation between being an undergraduate and a postgraduate. My father had slipped a disc, and in those days the cure was to lose weight. So he was put on a diet and my mother protested that she couldn't possibly cook all these different kinds of dishes, so I thought, well, actually, let's see what happens. I went on what, in fact, was the equivalent of an Atkins diet, and I lost three stones in three months – and this new, svelte thing emerged and then proceeded to throw himself around. Particularly after a term researching in Cambridge when it was off to London to do research on the big wide world, and fun was had by all. And that was why I was so determined to have my first job in London. And in many ways I was very lucky.

It was the late 1960s, early 1970s, and Gay Lib was really starting to hit – the scene was still quite bizarre. Places like the Catacombs in Earls Court. There were two big pubs in Earls Court

– there was also the Gigolo, which was the only bar in London where you could actually have sex. It had this strange little dance floor which everybody piled onto in such numbers that the gyrating was not particularly to the music. And, of course, there were the increasingly wonderful delights of Hampstead Heath. The upper parts of the Heath, just before coming down from what was then Jack Straw's Castle, were known by different names. Wankers Walk was one. There were scenes there that I can remember. One was almost magical: a kind of group sex in a ring, in a dell, on this evening where the temperature must have been in the high seventies.

You weren't ever tormented by your sexuality then?
No I wasn't. I think it was to do with the culture in which I'd been brought up. My mother was of course the standard puritan, but equally I was brought up on the basis of reasoned argument. I was only slapped twice, and I was an impossible child, as you can imagine; but my parents believed in argument. The schools that I went to were the same. If you did something, it was up to you to demonstrate if it was right or not. That then became the fundamental key really, not only to my attitude towards sexuality but to everything else – that you think about it, you debate it, you decide whether it's right or whether it's wrong. Years ago, with my first serious partner, a very bright lad called Jamie Gardner, who was an Australian maths student in London, much more heavily involved with gay politics than I was, we both asked ourselves why we didn't have these guilt feelings – and that's the answer. If you're taught that behaviour is a matter of reason and argument, it's no problem. If, though, you're told that sexuality emanates from divinely handed-down data, then you'll never escape it. So I was very fortunate.

Was coming out to your parents easy?
No, it wasn't. It was extremely difficult. And again, in retrospect, the whole coming out thing – there's an element of terrible self-indulgence: it's all about asserting one's own authenticity and rightness, and again there's an element of parade. There's an element of showing off. In my case it was not a thing to be very proud of at all. I think behind it was the quite deliberate intention of hurting my mother, and she made it all too easy and all too tempting. She was determined that I should marry, and that I should have two-and-a-half kids, and that I should lead a completely conventional life. And she neither understood nor forgave.

Also she felt that she had again produced a child who was not only physically disabled but was a kind of moral cripple. She also had terrible mental problems in her latter years. My father was completely different. For him it was worrying, perhaps more puzzling than anything else. It never occurred to him that chaps did that sort of thing. But he was always of the view that you tried to understand. And so he did his usual thing and went out and bought a lot of books on being gay. Absolutely terrific. And when a long, long time later, after my mother's death, and years after that even, when I transformed out of this monument to promiscuity and settled down with James, in the early 1990s, he was wonderful. He was then well into his eighties, but was welcoming, accepting and inviting. James and he got on incredibly well.

Did you have a role model? Someone in the public eye who helped you to come to terms with your sexuality?
No. There were all the Frankie Howerds and all the rest of the camp comics, like Kenneth Williams. With Gay Lib we all decided to be revolutionaries and start the world afresh. I've never been hugely influenced by role models. I've not modelled myself as a

historian on anybody; I certainly haven't modelled myself in the media on anybody. But what has always fascinated me as a gay person is the extent to which you have to be self-inventive: you invent yourself. You have taken a decision that breaks the rules. Therefore you either have no rules, like rather too many gay people, or you invent your own. And that very much has been my feeling throughout.

Were you involved in Gay Lib politics?
Only in the mildest kind of way. But what my sexuality did was to stop me from becoming what would otherwise have naturally happened to me – which is that I would have been a stuffed-shirt Cambridge don. That would have been my natural career, and the reason that that didn't happen was partly that Sir Geoffrey Elton was frightened of me, and was absolutely determined that I wasn't going to get a job at Cambridge where I was going to challenge him. But more importantly, I wanted to have fun in London. So I think the fact that I'm as maverick as I am, and slightly left field as I am, and as Channel 4 as I am, is entirely due to my sexuality. Absolutely without a doubt. And I think that as soon as we go on about how important it is that we be accepted, and become mainstream, we lose something, we lose the edge. Marginal groups are the creative groups. It's a standard historical phenomenon.

You were a member of TORCHE [Tory Campaign for Homosexual Equality]?
I was the first chairman and president. I am not a natural Tory at all, and indeed I have voted for the three main political parties. Throughout the 1960s I was absolutely solid Labour. I first voted Tory for the first Heath government, when he went to the country on the question, 'Who governs?' Later I thought Heath had been

such a catastrophe that I voted Liberal. And I only returned solidly to the Tories with Thatcher. And for me what I approved of with Thatcher was first of all that her high camp quality was quite wonderful, especially after she had received voice training, and had this swooping contralto, with the occasional turns of basso profundo when she really got going. She did utterly necessary things. She also broke down social barriers. I'd been brought up on a council estate and she transformed the hopes and aspirations of people living there. Some of it turned out to be fool's gold. But, hey, as somebody might say, that's politics.

The preceding Tory group, before TORCHE, was called, I think, the Conservative Campaign for Homosexual Equality. The new group got us a direct entrée to John Major at Downing Street. That whole business of McKellen and the meeting with Major took place, and at the Tory conference, in 1992 in Blackpool, where we had this extraordinary full debate. We hired this big room, and the Tory boys at last threw their brogues up in the air and came out. It was a quite extraordinary event. Matthew Parris was there, and he described it as one of the turning points in his life. Before that there was a time of conflict. But at least what happened was that it got the whole debate on the age of consent seriously going. It was reduced, though there was the absurd business of taking it down to 18. It produced that exchange between myself and Jeffrey Archer on *Question Time*, in which Archer leapt on his moral high horse, saying how absolutely intolerable it would be to take the homosexual age of consent down to the age of 16.

I'm afraid I just looked straight at camera and I said, 'Well, you know, what we've now got is a typical case of on the one hand this, on the other hand that, it's not going to be 21 but nor is it going to be 16, but I think the reason that Englishmen are so fond of sitting on the fence' – and I turned straight to Archer – 'is that they enjoy the sensation so much.' The audience erupted. It was a wonderful moment. But it began a serious debate and in a sense, in a funny kind of way, we were the first of the modernizers of the Tory Party.

At the same time, the Tories were responsible for the introduction of Section 28 . . .
I wouldn't get excited about Section 28.

Why not?
Because there are two aspects to it. One is that it was an attempt at the time to demonize; on the other hand, I don't think that public money should be spent endorsing anything – and that would apply to marriage too of course. These things seem to me to be essentially matters of private preference. The only legitimate concern that public policy has with these things is the cost of maintaining children if they don't have two parents. But these are not matters of morality, they're matters of public policy, and so I fail to get terribly excited about Clause 28. I think the whole gay and lesbian emphasis on the issue is ludicrous. I deeply dislike the way minorities become client groups for particular political interests – it's thoroughly unhealthy for politics, and it's thoroughly unhealthy for the minority groups. However, had I been Thatcher I wouldn't have touched Clause 28. She actually was perfectly relaxed on the subject. She's socially very liberal – after all, she married a divorced man. She's not an Ann Widdecombe, by any stretch of the imagination.

Did TORCHE debate Section 28?
Yes, it was debated quite extensively and we split – opinion was divided, but of course the moment the Labour government was returned, in a sense TORCHE became redundant. And being gay as a political issue has simply gone away, hasn't it? It really has.

I read an interview with you in which you said that on human rights New Labour is 'just words', and that all the changes they have made on the gay front are just 'right-on gestures'. Yet they scrapped Section 28, introduced civil partnership. Is that simply a gesture?
I think that whenever New Labour has made a liberal gesture, it is simply pandering to some particular focus group. It is a little bit of red meat thrown in the direction of its own left wing. I don't think there has been anything serious about it. If you actually look at its attitude to law, its attitude to social control, the actions over terrorism, the fact that you have a Labour Home Secretary saying that the one word that they can't stand is 'Liberalism', it seems to me my case is proven.

Human rights, gay rights, fox-hunting, these are things that Blair couldn't give a damn about. The only gays that Blair takes an interest in are celebs: the sort of thing Tony Blair cares about is gay celebrity – Elton John, Ian McKellen and the like.

I have absolutely no problem with the civil partnership thing at all; of course I haven't. I'm a huge believer in the right of the choice. What I would be deeply concerned about, however, is if we found ourselves in a position in which we started to establish the presumption that all relationships were to be given a legal dimension. I don't want a white wedding thank you very much. My sister-in-law, James's sister, is going through a wedding at the moment. The family eruptions, the nonsense, the tensions, every single dispute within the family is brought out, lovingly presented and dusted down. You don't want that! I really don't. Nor do I want the state interfering in my private life. I think generally it's the downside of acceptance. Do we really, when we consider the state of heterosexual marriage, want to go down that route? Do we really want to have a gay divorce crisis?

But would any of this have been achieved under a Tory government?
It would have probably split the party wouldn't it? I think that 18
was probably as far as they could have gone, and even that gave
poor old Ann Widdecombe paroxysms. When she was Hague's
home affairs spokeswoman in that election, I was entirely unable
to vote for the Conservative Party. I'm not a turkey voting for
Christmas, thank you very much. Let's again be quite clear, the
great problem for anybody who is a real liberal (as I regard myself
as being), is that the nineteenth-century liberal inheritance, for
bizarre reasons, went to the Left. It isn't naturally at home there.
The Labour Party is a natural managerial party: they believe in
big government, social engineering and intervention. And that's
not liberal, it's deeply illiberal – and the war on terror merely
provides another nice excuse.

On the other hand, economic liberalism rather bizarrely went
to the Conservative Party, and so if you are liberal, you find
yourself torn; and what I would like to see, of course, and what I
would hope will emerge from the current traumas of the Conservative Party is the old nineteenth-century Liberal Party – liberal
on social issues, and liberal economically.

*But what is it about parts of the Right that makes it resistant to
change, in terms of the gay issue?*
I think it's simply that they're conservative; for God's sake, what
does the word mean? There's also a religious flavour. They're conservative fundamentalists and their model is the Christian Right
in America. But I think in fact that the party grass roots have
changed enormously. These terribly grand, domineering ladies
that run the Tory Party on the whole adore these young gay men,
do they not? But you get a few people who don't, and there's
nothing very surprising about any of this. An awful lot of it is
justified in the name of protecting the family – but of course the

threat to the family isn't from gays, it's from the behaviour of heterosexual partners.

This year – and it's planned also for next – a Gay History Month has been established. This seems to be a project of writing a gay history, of gay lives and gay significance. Do you support that kind of activity?
I'm a bit dubious about it. It seems to me yet another splitting up of history into a mosaic, a mosaic reflecting, very unhelpfully, current concerns – so it's women, it's race, it's gay, it's working class. I think that's actually deeply unhelpful. I also think that the modern concept of homosexuality does not exist before the nineteenth century, and that therefore it is hugely distorting. Whatever James I thought he was, he did not think he was a homosexual. He undoubtedly lusted after boys. As I pointed out in my recent film, you can notice an appreciative royal glance towards the thighs of a male attendant in Rubens' apotheosis on the ceiling of the banqueting house. No doubt whatever, but he is not a modern gay.

What are the implications of teaching this in schools?
The implications are that it devalues history. It turns it merely into an endorsement for current concerns. Now I'm a huge believer in the relationship between past and present, and there's no doubt at all that the historian's role is to act as a kind of interpreter between past and present – you're explaining the one to the other. But if you let the whole balance fall over into the present, then it becomes ludicrous. Don't get me wrong, I've been one of the pioneers of talking frankly about people's sex lives. I wrote an entire book on it, about the six wives of Henry VIII, and one of the reviewers produced the wonderful line that Dr Starkey's favourite position is in the royal bedchamber, with a flashlight and a pair of binoculars. I'm not talking about suppressing it.

I see the fact that I'm gay as absolutely central to my identity. But it's not wholly me. It doesn't subsume or consume me, and this is what I get very worried about when people become professionally gay. I think it's something that's happened to Ian McKellen; you become professionally gay, you become professionally black. His Grace at York, he's black first and an archbishop second. And that I think is really, really dangerous.

Brian Paddick

The progress we have made in securing basic human rights in recent years through changes in legislation has been tremendous and well worth celebrating. Yet it is all too easy for those of us who mix with well-educated and liberal-minded people, gay and straight, for those of us who predominantly live, work and socialize in 'cosmopolitan' areas, for those of us in positions of authority within our chosen professions and for those of *you* whose chosen professions celebrate diversity, to believe that the world is an entirely different and welcoming place compared with what it was 20 years ago. Yet enjoying such a lifestyle is to be insulated from the challenges that many lesbian and gay people face who live in very different settings. Not that holding a senior position in an institution like the police service, which is routinely reviled for being too 'politically correct', is any protection. Although I count myself among the most privileged of LGBT people, working in a senior position in one of the most tolerant police services in the world, living in one of the most diverse capital cities in the world, and being able to choose some of the most broad-minded people to mix with, that is not to insulate me from attack simply for being who I am, a gay man holding the position I do as a Deputy Assistant Commissioner in the Metropolitan Police Service.

The Metropolitan Police included sexual orientation in its equal opportunities policy more than a decade ago, yet despite this, instances of alleged discrimination, both through formal organizational processes and by the actions of individuals, continue. It could be argued that in a police service attracting, as it does, greater and greater numbers of openly gay people, as well as some men and women who are transgender, an increase in reported discrimination is to be expected. Indeed, it is arguably a measure of the confidence that people from minority backgrounds have in their employer that they are prepared to report such incidents. That having been said, in a police service routinely condemned and praised in equal measure by different commentators for the undoubted progress it has made in the area of diversity, should not the corollary be an institution that is more tolerant, accepting (dare I say, even welcoming) of diversity within its workforce, resulting in fewer incidents of discrimination? While my favourite, perhaps the only, concept I remember from studying economics – *ceteris paribus* – is theoretically useful, in real life it is not possible to hold all other variables constant in order to decide whether, in this case, an increase in reported discrimination is a good thing or a bad thing.

The way in which discrimination manifests itself and is experienced can vary depending on who you are, how you fit with the prevailing organizational culture and where you are in the organization. Towards the top of the police service the issues become more political: there is still active debate among some as to whether being gay, or even supporting openly gay staff, can damage a senior officer's ability to lead an organization. Some still believe (wrongly in my opinion) that the Metropolitan Police, to take a specific example, is predominantly homophobic, in that the majority of rank and file police officers are believed to be openly hostile to, and many senior officers covertly against, homosexuality in general, and lesbians and gays in the police in particular.

When a mixture of truth and lies about my 'private life' was made public, it was the damage this had allegedly done to my ability to lead the police officers and staff under my command that was the primary reason put forward by those questioning my suitability to continue in office. Interestingly, similar revelations about a straight senior officer would arguably have had the opposite effect in the prevailing culture of the police service, confirming him to be 'one of the lads' (unless he was a she, in which case she would be condemned as the 'station bike'). These negative perceptions of straight women and gay men and the relatively positive perceptions of straight men and lesbians betray the negative police stereotypes of 'gays' as 'effeminate' and 'dykes' as 'butch' in what is still a predominantly macho police culture.

A clear illustration of the prevailing culture in the police service is the way officers react to being asked about their home lives. I try to show my genuine interest in colleagues by asking them about both their professional and their family lives, always ensuring they are happy to discuss them with me. Straight officers usually name their partners, volunteer the names and ages of their children, sometimes even producing photographs, despite the fact that I, as a gay man with no children, have little or nothing in common with them as far as my family life is concerned. A few years ago I was conducting a review which involved me speaking to a number of middle-ranking police officers. In the 'getting to know them as a person' sessions, some of the officers very clumsily avoided any gender-specific references to their partners. When I suggested I may have seen one of them before, the officer coloured with embarrassment and shyly suggested it may have been at a 'social event' (guardedly referring to a Gay Police Association 'drop-in'). If middle-ranking police officers are afraid to talk about their same-sex partners to an openly gay, albeit senior, colleague, what does this say about how comfortable even leaders within the police service feel about being 'out' at work?

Among those police officers and staff towards the lower levels in the organization, discrimination is felt more directly in terms of comments, blatant and subtle, spoken or scrawled on lockers and payslips, from both colleagues and members of the public. While comments about Sir Ian McKellen are not routinely prefaced by the word 'gay actor', police colleagues who are open about their sexuality tell me how they are often referred to as 'the gay officer' by the public. This to me demonstrates the general acceptability, even presumption, of homosexuality in some professions while our presence in other roles ranges from being 'noteworthy' to 'outrageous', even where, as in the case of the police service, it has never been a legal disqualification from holding the office of constable.

The decision to make my sexuality known publicly was taken in conjunction with the most senior officers in the Metropolitan Police Service. On the second anniversary of the publication of the Mcpherson Report into the tragic death of Stephen Lawrence, the Service wanted to prove its diversity credentials. It proposed to the *Guardian* that it run an article featuring three high-ranking police officers: one female, one black and one gay. I used to tell colleagues the story and ask them to guess which of the three I was going to be. The story was turned down by the *Guardian* but a reporter from *The Financial Times* was given the go-ahead to interview me on progress in race relations in the police since Stephen Lawrence's death, and to drop into the middle of the article the fact that I was the most senior openly gay police officer in the UK. The Commissioner was concerned that we should manage my 'outing' rather than risk my being 'outed' at a time that would have been difficult for me professionally. From that Saturday edition of the other 'Pink Paper', almost every newspaper article on whatever subject involving me was prefaced with 'Brian Paddick, the most senior openly gay police officer . . .'

In terms of support for lesbian and gay staff, again experiences differ. Traditionally, where a senior police officer is 'in trouble', he (usually) derives his support from other senior colleagues, who tend to stick together in times of difficulty, particularly when the attack is from outside the police service (such as the support David Westwood, Chief Constable of Humberside, received when attacked over the handling of information about Ian Huntley, the school caretaker who killed schoolgirls Holly Wells and Jessica Chapman). Rank and file officers, on the other hand, tend to be supported by their 'trade union', the Police Federation, where the 'attack' usually comes in the form of disciplinary action taken against their members by senior police officers. The perceived lack of support from the Police Federation for lesbian and gay officers, particularly in discrimination cases, and a general sense of vulnerability felt by lesbians and gays in the police, resulted in the formation of the Lesbian and Gay Police Association (a 'support' organization, not a representative body, as the only representative body for rank and file police officers allowed by law is the Police Federation). Having been formally established in 1990, the Gay Police Association as it is now known (many female members apparently not wanting to be called 'lesbian', another manifestation of the macho police culture perhaps) does excellent work with LGBT police officers and police staff, providing help and advice, usually to rank and file officers who find themselves unfairly subjected to disciplinary action by their senior police colleagues.

What then happens when it is a senior gay police officer who comes under attack from outside the police service and is simultaneously subjected to a disciplinary investigation? In my case, the traditional personal support from other senior police colleagues was almost totally absent, with one notable exception – a very senior colleague who had recently moved to another force who called on the day the trouble started. They would not even pick up the telephone in circumstances where only the caller and I would have known of their support; although to be fair, halfway into the eight-month enquiry, when it was becoming clear that the case against me would fail, Sir John (now Lord) Stevens did call me at home to see how I was. Being close to the top of the organization, a combination of hierarchical distance and the predominant Gay Police Association caseload of supporting the junior officer against 'the bosses' resulted in a breakdown in communication between me and the Gay Police Association. Remarkably, it was external support, the avalanche of supportive letters and cards from members of the public, dozens of MPs signing an Early Day Motion in the House of Commons condemning the way I was being treated by the police, and the 5,000-signature petition demanding my rein-statement, even a 'Lambeth4Paddick' website, which added to my determination to fight and win.

Police officers, like members of the armed forces and civil servants, are legally 'crown servants' and not employees. Prior to the inclusion of sexual orientation in the legal framework in relation to employment on 1 December 2003 (The Employment Equality [Sexual Orientation] Regulations 2003), lesbian and gay police officers were in a particularly weak position. Except where laws state 'for the purpose of this legislation, police officers are to be treated as if they were employees', police officers are not covered by employment legislation. While legal redress for dis-crimination on the grounds of sex and race has been available to police officers since the introduction of the Sex Discrimination Act and the Race Relations Act, broader employee protection, for example against unfair or constructive dismissal, even now is still not available to police officers. When I believed that I was being discriminated against by the Metropolitan Police on the basis of my sexual orientation, prior to the changes in legislation, I had one of my briefest ever meetings with a solicitor. I was told that, as a police officer who believed I had been discriminated against because I was gay, I had no legal rights, end of story.

The history of the Metropolitan Police is littered with alleged race and sex discrimination cases brought by members of staff. A series of high-profile Employment Tribunal cases resulted in highly damaging opening statements on behalf of aggrieved black and female police officers being covered in the media. Even in instances where the case was subsequently decided in the police's favour, the damage to the Met's reputation had been done, with the final result receiving little or no publicity. The Metropolitan Police has since adopted a policy of settling cases out of court wherever possible. Now cases tend to be fought to the eleventh hour and then, in increasing numbers, settled with five-figure *ex gratia* payments, carefully crafted words of apology and promises to accommodate the officer's future career ambitions. Prior to the legislative changes, with no legal levers to pull and no access to Employment Tribunal, gay and lesbian officers were unable to secure such redress for what appeared to be clear instances of unfair treatment. In my case, after over a year of argument and an independent review of the way I was treated, a letter of apology was the only recompense I was able to secure.

I am not exactly clear what the right-wing agenda is around lesbians and gay men in positions of authority. Quite plainly right-wingers do not approve, or at least they do not approve when you are open about your sexuality; a columnist in a right-wing Sunday tabloid proclaimed that by coming out, the first openly gay Conservative MP had given up all right to the protection of the party (implying that if he had stayed in the closet, he would have been all right). Perhaps there is something about the police service in particular, seen by some as guardians of the *status quo*, conservative with a small 'c', obedient servants to their political masters, which makes having innovative and 'unconventional' people in senior positions unpalatable, even contradictory.

My own induction into this mentality began after I had met a right-wing columnist at a debate on the legalization of cannabis when he called to say how good it was to meet me. While he was on the telephone, could he check a few facts? 'It's true, is it not, that you are a homosexual?' Having said that I was, his newspaper's search for a damaging story had begun.

Some six months later, my ex-wife called me to tell me that journalists from the same newspaper had called at her home asking to speak to her about me. She refused to talk to them. Six months after that, following payment of £100,000 to a former partner whom I had separated from some 15 months before, two simultaneous 'exclusives' appeared in page after page of two Sunday tabloids. A mixture of lies and intimate details of my private life, from where I bought my suits to my HIV status (how many times has that figured in a 'straight' kiss-and-tell story?), resulted in a nine-month investigation into minor drugs allegations, which were clearly not provable from the start. I was removed from my position as the police commander in Lambeth, South London. The investigation eventually concluded that, even if I had done anything wrong, it was not sufficiently serious to warrant any formal punishment (not even a reprimand).

Despite the exoneration and a public campaign, I was not allowed to return to my post. A series of 'back office' roles followed. When I was eventually promoted by the Metropolitan Police Authority, an anonymous source at Scotland Yard was quoted in a national newspaper as saying it was 'too soon after the investigation' for me to be promoted. The appointment of Sir Ian Blair as Commissioner of the Metropolitan Police coincided with my being posted to the first key position I had held in the Met since my removal from Lambeth some three years previously. A long and potentially financially ruinous legal action against the main tabloid concerned in the 'kiss-and-tell' story resulted in substantial compensation, the payment of costs and an apology printed in the newspaper.

With the best of intentions, being open about my sexuality had opened the floodgates to a sneering, insidious form of discrimination, cleverer and more difficult to pin down or battle against. When I represented the police service at the 2004 Liberal Democrat Party Conference, engaging in a panel debate on law and order, one tabloid newspaper felt the need to comment on my 'designer suit' and the fact that, in their opinion, I was sitting with my legs 'as wide apart as possible' but without reference to anything I said. The headline 'He Strutted Across the Stage Like a Game Show Host', deliberately placed immediately above my name, was a quote from the article, but one that did not refer to me at all. The cynical juxtaposition of headlines or articles is common practice in some tabloid newspapers.

Further attempts to undermine and ridicule continue. In the summer of 2005 I was asked by the Commissioner, Sir Ian Blair, to conduct a review of the way the Metropolitan Police investigate (all) rape in London, as rape investigation is one of the many types of crime investigation for which I have responsibility in London. This led a tabloid newspaper to comment negatively on me, my professionalism and my sexuality. The newspaper columnist stated that, even though I had been cleared, I should have been punished for those things I had been accused of by my disgruntled former partner and I had only been promoted because I was gay. Two weeks later, when terrorists exploded four bombs in London killing over 60 people, I was responsible for reassuring Londoners and those around the world, representing the Metropolitan Police in a series of press conferences.

Rather than comment on the messages I had delivered on behalf of the Metropolitan Police, further negative references to my sexuality and the allegations made by my former partner followed, the day after the bombings and the next day. The response from the public was interesting. Many e-mails were complimentary, about both the content of what I had said and the manner of delivery. Three anonymous letters, no doubt prompted by the tabloid's references to my sexuality, were homophobic, deeply offensive and distressing, particularly to my personal staff who had opened and read the letters. One included graphic references to sexual practices and a distorted view of their consequences. To their credit, the Metropolitan Police Service investigated each of these malicious communications to their fullest extent.

Is there still residual homophobia in the police service? Selection for promotion is always a double-edged sword for people from minorities. In promotion competitions in any organization, you often get a large number of very able applicants for a few senior positions. In such situations it is all too easy to identify some minor point as the reason for selecting another candidate rather than the underlying homophobia that actually determines the decision in some people's minds. I was fortunate enough to have been promoted through the ranks using an objective assessment centre process involving a number of exercises marked by a series of assessors. Promotions are now based on one or two interviews where, with the best will in the world, personal prejudice can determine the outcome. Conversely, in an open and fair competition, where the objectively best candidate is from a minority background, the accusation is often made that the decision was a 'politically correct' one, because of the person's sexuality, for example, and nothing to do with merit. The fact that six out of my seven promotions took place before I was open about my sexuality does not stop homophobes from accusing me of only being in the position I hold because I am gay.

The police service generally and the Metropolitan Police in particular have made considerable progress towards ensuring equality of opportunity and equity in treatment of people both within their own ranks and in the service they deliver to the public. This is not about political correctness nor is it just about morality and the defence of the human rights of minorities. It is about delivering an appropriate, an equitable, an equally beneficial police service to everyone in society. It is about ensuring that the best people, whoever they are and whatever their background, belief, or sexual orientation, reach the very top of their chosen profession, to the benefit of all those within that profession and the recipients of the service delivered by that profession. It is also sound business sense to encourage those with an alternative view, whose criticism of the *status quo* is intended to be a positive attempt to improve the organization to which they belong, rather than a cynical attempt to cause damage. Complaints are opportunities to develop and evolve. Compliments can be seen as reasons to stagnate. Instances of homophobia perpetrated by police officers are still reported by members of staff and members of the public. These incidents are not as frequent as they have been in the past, but at the same time they are still occurring. In my opinion, the police service is half-way along its journey towards equality of opportunity: it's OK to be 'different' in the police, provided you behave like a straight white man! We need to move from a position where diversity is tolerated to one where diversity is celebrated.

Stewart Brown

I'm originally from the west of Scotland, a place called Helens-burgh, but I was brought up in a place called Linwood, which is a very old industrial town. The old Chrysler factory used to be there, and after they left in 1981 it became a bit of a ghost town. I was four when I moved there in 1974. I stayed until I was 24. I'm 35 now. Still a bit of a mummy's boy. Just too scared to leave.

Was it easy to come out to your parents?
Yes. Dead easy. I only came out to myself in March 1989, after a long period of thinking. It goes back to when I was about 12. I vaguely remember having some sort of feelings for a friend of mine. It was just a boyish 12-year-old thing. Nothing ever happened. Over my teenage years I used to sit and watch TV and be attracted to men. I used to try and put all those thoughts to one side and try and forget about it. I've met a lot of people over the last 20 years whose experiences of that type were harrowing or quite difficult for them. But for me it was a bit of fun.

There was a period at school of being bullied, but I got through it OK. I enjoyed all those camp figures on television, like John Inman. Boy George had a great influence on my thinking about being gay and being open. Building up to coming out wasn't difficult. It was just a time of great thinking for me. It didn't cause me a lot of sleepless nights.

You were aware of the scene?
I was going out with a girl, Julia, from Essex and we broke up halfway through a skiing holiday. Then I was getting the bus home from King's Cross and just walking about, and I went to a

newsagent's stall and bought a copy of *Gay Times* and had the most fantastic bus journey home ever. That was my first experience of learning a lot of things that I never knew before, and there was a directory at the back that showed me exactly where to go in Glasgow. So I knew there must be a gay scene of some sort.

You didn't really know any other gay people at that time?
No, not one person. I told my mum about a week before I started my fire service training and she hugged me, said 'I don't care what you're doing as long as you're being careful, as long as you're being safe'. Then off I went to do my 16-week residential fire service training. I used to come home at weekends.

Was that far from home?
Yes, it was in the east side of Scotland in a place called Gullen, in East Lothian. Just before I went out there I met a guy, who was my first relationship. Almost immediately I went to do my training, so it was difficult, but it also had a positive side because there was something to look forward to when I came home.

Did you carry on that relationship throughout your training?
Yes. It was good for me because he was ten years older and knew a lot about gay life, and so became a bit of a mentor for me, taking me under his wing. I did my training and continued this relationship for nine months and after that we split up.

What attracted you to the fire service?
Big red fire engines and big red hoses.

In terms of the culture of the fire service, is it 'macho'?
Yes, big time.

All the way up the hierarchy?
It's always been like that. White male heterosexual. The fire service is based on traditions that come out of the Royal Navy. For instance, the watches: the red watch, the blue watch, the white watch. They all come from naval traditions. It used to be very militaristic. We had to wear uniform and salute.

Did you know before that it was going to be like that?
I had done a lot of research on the fire service before I joined, so yes. I had a two-year period between leaving school and joining the fire service, bumming about and doing a few jobs, and during that time I visited a few fire stations. Training school was tough in respect of all that militaristic ideology. The way the service was run was very antiquated because all fire service senior managers were ex-servicemen, so you basically became a firefighter, climbing the ranks, becoming chief fire officer eventually if you wanted to.

It was male, straight. At that time they still didn't know about me. I was leading a double life but it was cool. You get to know everyone else's most intimate secrets because for some bizarre reason within those four walls people just sit and talk about the most bizarre things and don't actually realize what they're talking about. But I didn't want to open myself up to all this.

So were you quiet . . .
Yes, though I was known as a bit of a cheeky lad; but that was a defence mechanism, to try and keep them away from prying too much. And it worked for a certain period of time, and then it all just collapsed! A guy off another watch caught me close to a cruising area in Glasgow. I was walking along the road from the bushes, and he walked up to me and said 'Ooh, what are you doing up there?', because it was in a part of town where there was no other reason for me to be up, apart from maybe playing

football, and he knew that I wasn't a big football fan. And it was so annoying that, when I got back to the station, I knew that people had been talking about me.

They were being playful, but they were being nasty about it as well because they had found out that they had a gay guy on the shift. My shift had quite a few people at the top of the ladder who ruled the roost, and I was right at the bottom at that stage. People at the top used to manipulate the people in the middle to try and bully the ones at the very bottom. That's how it worked. But I fought back after a long time and I managed to kind of break down that system. Eventually I got to know everybody very well and they liked me. We used to play golf and socialize together.

So it didn't really become an issue?
They weren't really that bothered about it, although for two months after it came out, it was bad for me. After that it was completely fine and quite a few people actually became a lot closer to me. They tended, unofficially, to take me under their wing and make sure I was OK, and I really was thankful for it, because I knew full well that there could have been a situation where it would have been ten times worse and I could have been bullied, harassed, forced to leave the job, or at worst, take my own life. I have met people who have been in those situations in brigades, because of the culture. And it has never really changed that much. Out of 49,500 firefighters in the UK, we have only 350 people on our database of the gay support network that I run. I know for a fact that there must be another few hundred.

What then about your sexuality politicized you?
I think it was the fact that while trade unions had embraced equality, they were a long, long way behind other organizations in terms of equality issues, and they wanted to learn more at that time.

Your group operates within the trade union?
Yes. There was need for a support network within the union and I was introduced to the London representatives.

Were you involved in rolling it out nationally then?
It was a haphazard approach initially because the union didn't want to throw it at the membership and then have the membership throw it back and say 'We don't want to do this'. So it was done very slowly, from 1994 to about 1997. Then the union just put out a simple flyer every four months to fire stations which said that the union had established a network for gay and lesbian firefighters. They set up a confidential phone number and gradually people started to get in touch. We had a huge education programme in the union and used to go round to the regions and to the brigades, and do three-day seminars.

For everyone?
Well, for people who wanted to go on them. It wasn't forced. Most people treat a trade union as their insurance policy, in case their employer attacks them in any way. So basically it was done through workshops where you can learn about equal opportunities, you can learn about a whole raft of issues. There were a few seminars where we had tutors who were well up on gay and lesbian issues; a session, for example, on gay and lesbian history, and the union would invite me to come up and speak to these seminars. The executive council of the union had brought forward a rule-change to bring in to the main structure of the union a national gay and lesbian committee, a national women's committee, and a national black and ethnic minority members committee, so that was integrated into the main body of the structure of the union.

Have you encountered any kind of hostilities to that?
Yes: huge amounts.

What, within stations?
It was 'Well, the fire brigade has always been a white male culture, why are you trying to change it?' You know, it's a man's job. That kind of attitude. If it's a man's job then there's no place for women in the job, no place for blacks, and certainly none for gays. That's the way society has been in this country. The police is the same, the army is the same. Employers and managers and people within the union want to modernize, and get people to realize that society has changed.

Back in 1999, a report on equality in the fire service said that the most difficult task faced by the fire service in advancing equality and fairness was moving opinion and understanding on the issue of sexuality. But it also said it was unsafe to be open about sexuality.
The unsafe side of things was that they didn't feel that the fire service had changed culturally enough for gay men to be safe in those environments. And that's why, to a certain extent, the job was changed. It was unsafe in a way that meant that gays could be bullied, harassed or beaten up.

Even in 1999?
Yes. But there was no follow-on from it. It was unsafe and it was a taboo subject. Full stop. There were no recommendations to take forward as to how they were going to address the situation, the underlying problem of how to deal with the subject of having gay men in the fire service.

Is that where you came in?
We came in very quickly and introduced a committee called the Equal Opportunities Task Group, made up of stakeholders, the trade unions, the employers, the Local Government Association,

together with the Home Office, chief fire officers, and the minority sections of the fire brigade union. They recommended a way forward to modernize the fire service, and I got involved after about a year or so of that committee meeting. We have done a lot of things over the years. We managed to persuade them to bring in HIV/AIDS policies that they would never have had before, an HIV/AIDS health and safety policy, not only raising awareness of the issue, but also dealing with someone who might have or is perceived to have HIV in the workplace, and dealing with members of the public who are HIV if you have to administer first aid. In 2000, the national gay and lesbian committee put together a policy in conjunction with the National AIDS Trust, and got all the fire authorities to sign up to it. I've just got all 58 authorities to sign up to the Stonewall Diversity Champions programme.

What help came from the government?
There doesn't seem to be much joined-up thinking in government departments, and that has become clearer as time has moved on. When we first got involved, we were under the Home Office, then we moved to the DTLR (Department for Transport, Local Government and the Regions), which was part of the local government in the regions, then we were shoved into the Office of the Deputy Prime Minister. It just seemed that nobody wanted the fire service. It was difficult to deal with. The trade union was very strong. I think over the years the stuff that the government has done with regard to equality legislation has helped, but to this day, managers in the fire service – and I mean managers who were ex-firefighters and have moved up the ranks – don't seem to embrace legislation as much as they could have done.

There's so much the government could have done to educate fire service employers, managers, employees, about being gay in the fire service. They could have gone to Stonewall, and easily stuck two or three million pounds into Stonewall's budget and said, 'Go and help the fire service.' At one point they were talking about putting role models out – folk like myself – in a full-time job. I didn't want that at that time. I was still working as a firefighter as well as doing my trade union duties. I didn't want to be taken out of the fire station life and be thrown into going every day to different fire stations, saying 'I'm gay, here's my story'. I've done it a few times, and after giving your story a couple of times, it becomes pretty dull. I did an interview for a magazine called *Base* up in Scotland about two months ago, and that was pretty cool. But if you're sat in a fire station talking about yourself, it becomes really uncomfortable.

Were they interested?
Some of them were OK. Some of them sat there and said, 'I don't really care if you're gay. If you worked on my shift I wouldn't care', and that was fine; but I couldn't do it on a day-to-day basis. I think that's what the government was looking to do at the time, but it never materialized. There were no support networks put in place around the country for people who were coming out. There were no policies to say 'This is how managers should support people if they come out; if they come out and they are being bullied and harassed, this is what you should do.' I wanted to get each fire authority set up with a point of contact straight to the chief, or at least to the deputy chief.

So has much changed?
There are 58 authorities and a number of them have the resources to move forward. The London authority has had positive action days, as has the West Midlands, and I think the Lothian and Borders and Greater Manchester branches have as well. It's a long-drawn-out process, but I feel we are slowly changing people's minds. And we promote a positive image of gays in the

fire service now, at Pride events up and down the country, which basically say that it's OK and cool to join the fire service as a gay man, a lesbian or trans-sexual.

Was your group in 2005's Pride March in London?
Yes, since 1999 we've either marched with the banner that you can see on our website, or with a fire engine. At the last one, I was sitting on top of the fire engine. It has been fairly high profile, but it has tailed off slightly recently, and the police have taken over, because you see them there all in line, marching up and down in their uniforms.

One of the most frustrating things for me is that the police can co-ordinate their effort when it comes to the Gay Pride events and they're also getting funded. The government, for instance, funds the Gay Police Association, while the funding for the fire brigade union comes from membership. At the moment we have to be careful about the amount we are spending as we are short of money because of the dispute. If our fire service dispute about pay had gone on another month, the union would have been bankrupt, that's how bad it was. As a committee we decided that we'd hit Brighton, London and Birmingham Prides this year.

You're not fighting fires at present, but can you tell me about the stereotypical images of firemen that you enjoy?
Yes, there's always a good side to a job like this. For instance, the way that the public perceives you is fantastic. The public image of firefighters is great. After coming out, I got into situations where I would just drive about, not making it too obvious that I was actually following men. It was good because there were always some nice-looking men, and there were a couple of nice-looking girls, so the guys in the back would say 'She's fit.' And so I'd be looking at the men. There was one occasion where a couple of guys had handcuffed a mate to some railings in the town centre as

part of a stag night. He was naked and absolutely gorgeous. We drove past and I just got to the end of the road and doubled back, and everyone said, 'Where you going?' I said, 'I'm going back to help him.' 'He doesn't need help,' they replied. And I said 'I'M GOING BACK TO HELP HIM!'

I do regret my current detachment from the fire station, but there are things I certainly won't miss, like being in a single dormitory with 16 other men . . .

Isn't that changing?
Different fire brigades work in different ways. For instance, they obviously have separate facilities for females nowadays. The dormitories are huge rooms. You can imagine being in on a Friday or Saturday night and having to sleep in these rooms with a load of other men who are all snoring. It's not nice.

Not the fantasy image then?
Definitely not. It's not great hunks of men walking into bed with Calvin Klein pants on. Most are overweight.

The London Fire Service has sometimes been criticized for being decades behind the police in terms of combating homophobia in its ranks. Is this true?
As far as the recruitment side of things is concerned, where you get a panel of fire service managers who are officers, if they had an inclination that you were gay, you would probably get a cross against your name, which would prevent you from getting promotion.

The good reputation of the police has resulted in part from correcting the bad relations which they had with gay communities when they enforced homophobic laws, and so on. The fire service doesn't play that kind of role in people's lives. But it's true that we haven't moved on as much as the police in promoting a positive

image for gays in the service. And I just put it down to funding –
it's purely and utterly about funding, and also the motivation of
either ministers or civil servants about how they want to promote
the fire service. You don't have to be Einstein to work it out: in the
public's eyes, the police have to be modernized, and that mod-
ernization will take on large issues. The fire service, by contrast, is
a public service like the prison service that's perhaps held back
from the public eye. There's no real incentive to promote the fire
service in the same way as the police service.

*How much longer will it take to eradicate prejudice against gays in the
fire service?*
I foresee big changes in the next decade. There's a bit of a
momentum at the moment, and I think in the next few years, if we
see some high-profile legal cases emanating from the sexual orientation regulations, you will see a change in the way of thinking.
But there are always senior officers who will turn round and say,
'We don't have to worry because we've got sexual orientation in
our equal opportunities policy', and you feel like telling them that
that policy's not worth the paper it's written on.

Are you going to take advantage of the civil partnership legislation?
I've really worked hard in the trade union movement to bring
about that kind of legislation, and I'm really glad it's there. I'm not
desperate to take up on it. I'm very happy in my personal situation
at present. I think the one thing that might make my attitude
towards that change, is that at the moment I can't leave my pension
to my partner Ian. In the past the government has made a lot of
money from pensions reverting to them when one half of a gay
partnership dies, and that's certainly been the case in the fire
service. So I'll probably be tempted to take advantage of that.

Credit: Miki Slingsby

Maggi Hambling

People describe me as over the top, but nobody's ever told me what the top is that I'm supposed to be over. I mean, what is the top? Have a bit of fun! Have a laugh! If you're camp, be very camp. If you're butch, be very butch.

When people started to use the word 'gay', it did seem a bit nonsensical. I know there's a lot of good work to be done, but people get so earnest. Derek Jarman, who was a great friend of mine, always said, 'You've got to say queer, gay is sort of polite.' There's a wonderful thing in one of his obituaries. He said it wasn't that straight people were normal, merely rather common.

I was a bit of a 'mixed infant', I'd say. My best friend was the boy next door called Rex. Every day of the holidays we'd have a fight to decide who would be Robin Hood and who would be Maid Marian. And guess who was always Robin Hood? I think he went on to be queen of the Ipswich School.

My brother and sister were eleven and nine years older than me. My brother definitely wanted a brother, so when my mother came back from the hospital with me, she had to admit I was a girl rather than a boy. He decided to ignore that technicality.

When I was once given a doll, we immediately took it to the woodshed and carved it up. He taught me carpentry and wringing chickens' necks and the usual sort of things. And so I really was brought up as a boy. Then, when he was a teenager, he started French-kissing me, which didn't really work.

And my father – though I didn't know this until later in life – was bisexual. Very proper behind the *Daily Telegraph*, but quite capable, when in the company of farm labourers, of becoming quite feminine. Much later in life, when he retired from banking, I gave him some paints and he started to paint, and that brought us together – he had been distant throughout my childhood.

When I was a child, my mother was both mother and father. She used to visit Women's Institutes to demonstrate ballroom dancing and she took me as her partner. She led as the man. Country life in Suffolk was strange.

I was the second head of the John Hitchcock gang. When John Hitchcock was ill, I was gang leader. We had real battles. There was a sloping lawn with high banks on both sides going down into a valley. One gang would be on either side and we'd charge down and meet in armed combat. If we took prisoners, we tortured them. Poor Rex! We often caught Rex. We would tie him down to a great big dead tree and torture him.

But, because I had the longest blondest hair and the loudest voice, I was always the Virgin Mary in the nativity play. It would have left most children in a bit of a muddle.

Much later in life, when I went on buses I remember one day being appalled. A boy was sitting by himself, and all the other schoolboys were jolly and happy and suddenly one of them said: 'Ugh, don't sit beside him. He's a queery. He's a queery.' Like that. Tiny boys. I was shocked by the age of these boys and that they even knew the word 'queer'. Bullying clearly does go on in schools. Trying to stop it is an important part of the work of Stonewall.

I had a very close liaison with a girl two years below me at school. I remember going back to her house for tea one day and she took me up to the bedroom and took off her school uniform and danced naked in front of me and I got very, very excited. But I didn't know quite what to do about it.

And in my girls' school in Suffolk, there was this music mistress who wore a three-cornered hat, like Napoleon, and a tie. Several teachers wore ties and tweed suits and sat with their legs apart. They marched along the lunch-queue telling us not to touch each other. Very paranoid. And one schoolmistress was sacked for having a close relationship with the hockey captain.

My mother didn't take kindly to my being queer. After I told her, I didn't go home to see my parents for a very long while. And I wrote them a letter saying 'If you can't accept me as I am, then I'm very sorry.'

My mother was a very churchy person. She eventually went on a retreat to a monastery. One day the organizers put up a sign saying 'If you have anything you'd like to discuss in private with a monk, just let us know'. So my mother had a private chat. She told the monk that one of her daughters was married but the other was a lesbian. He told her sternly that he hoped she'd never blamed me for it and he prayed that she hadn't stopped showing her love. Bless him. It changed my mother completely. She came back from that trip and it was never the issue it was before. Perhaps he was queer.

When I was a student at Camberwell in the 1960s (when censorship and all that went) we had a 'gay' table (we used the word 'gay' then) in the canteen, and wouldn't let people sit down unless they were gay. But we had two friends, Antoinette and Robin, who were straight but very glamorous, like film stars. So we did let them sit down.

I get my energy from just being alive. A lot of the time one is in doubt about one's work. Doom, gloom, despair. Like many creative people, I can be a bit of a manic-depressive. As high as a kite about my work for a moment, or much more often in the pits of despair.

So I do need a drink in the evening. I go pottier than ever if I don't work for a day-and-a-half. Pottier than I am already. When things go right, it's an incredible feeling. But often I've worked three months on something and it comes to life and dies and comes to life and dies and finally *does* die. Then it has to be destroyed with a knife and got rid of.

Then, with a bit of luck that painting can happen very quickly on a new canvas, but it wouldn't have been able to happen if I hadn't been buggering around doing it wrong for three months. The most difficult decision in the whole thing is knowing when to stop. That's the most difficult. But artists are very lucky. Instead of murdering someone, for instance, they have the possibility of making a painting of the murder. Or writing a poem, or creating a piece of music. Having a channel of expression is where artists are very lucky indeed.

Coming out? I've never been in. And victims of bullying should get some muscles! Or make people laugh! And be proud! They should be proud!

Alan Hollinghurst

I was born in Stroud, in Gloucestershire. My father was a bank manager so we moved around a bit, first to Faringdon in Berkshire for eight years, and then to Cirencester. My father died 15 years ago, but my mother still lives there. And I still think of the Cotswold part of Gloucestershire as my home landscape.

Did you enjoy rural life?
I have deep feelings about it. That landscape is hauntingly beautiful, and it has a wonderfully rich and harmonious building tradition: those things are very deep in my system somehow. I'm usually very moved when I visit it, but I have to admit that after a few days I feel a keen urge to get back to town. There's a quite disproportionate sense of relief when I turn off the M40 on to the North Circular. Though I don't believe in such stuff, I seem to be a textbook Geminian, and I feel this geographical thing like a tug between two different parts of my personality.

That was what *The Spell* was about in a way: the middle-aged gay man trying to settle down in the country, and the younger actor boyfriend who doesn't take to the idea at all well. Robin, the oldest of the quartet of characters in the book, is an architect who comes from the West Country originally, moves to London, but then buys and does up a beautiful old cottage in Dorset, as the setting for a fantasy of the idyllic life.

You went to school in Dorset?
Yes, a school called Canford. I first went away to a prep school in Berkshire, when I was seven, and then on to Canford when I was thirteen. My first ten days at prep school I cried virtually non-stop,

but then suddenly decided that actually it wasn't too bad. In fact after that I was nearly always very happy at school.

I was always very excited by buildings. Both my boarding schools were in beautiful old country houses; my prep school was in a Jacobean house, and Canford was a Victorian gothic mansion designed by Barry just after his great triumph with the Palace of Westminster. It seemed to me imaginatively quite rich, though this was by no means a common view among the other boys. I lived a sort of fantasy life in these houses, almost as if they were mine; in a way it was a bit like the Freudian idea of the family romance, the idea that really you belong to some quite other family, that you're a kind of changeling. This fantasy of possession is something I tried to objectify in Nick in *The Line of Beauty*.

And it was all boys?
Yes.

Was it at school that you first experienced curiosity and attraction to other boys?
It certainly was.

How old were you?
I suppose at puberty, which with me I think was relatively early, at about 11 or so. I remember it being intensely absorbing, the sense of change and novelty and exploration. It was like being admitted to a further dimension. It was completely natural, but in its context it was made to feel very naughty. I was always very happy at home with my parents in the holidays, but over those years I began to feel more and more urgently that school was somewhere I wanted to get back to. It was terribly exciting to get back to school, and see the boys, a few of them in particular.

Was sexuality ever a problem?
It certainly wasn't at my prep school. At Canford it was a bit different. The school was founded in the 1920s, and while it imitated a lot of the rules and rituals and arcane names for things that you might have in a really old public school, it didn't have any corresponding tradition of sexual behaviour. What went on was mainly on the border between ragging and sex. Maybe I just missed out, but I think it was quite unusual for people to have real sexual relations, and the prevailing attitude to such things was fairly disapproving and middle class. Of course school life was shot through with sexual emotions, but there was so much unease and denial associated with them that you couldn't do anything too earnestly or wholeheartedly.

Had you a sense of what it was like to be a gay man in the society in which you grew up?
I was a teenager in the 1960s and early 1970s, and don't remember feeling the encouragement of any strong unambiguous role models at all. My schools were country schools, pretty effectively isolated from the currents of the outside world. We joked about some of the masters and some of the boys, but I don't suppose I actually met and talked to an out gay man until my first year at Oxford. At home the subject seemed even more remote: my parents had no gay friends or acquaintances. There was no one else gay in the family. No positive or practical image of gayness existed in the world I moved in. At best there was occasional rather risqué talk about Tchaikovsky, or Noël Coward. As an only child I think I was perhaps more tolerant of this socio-sexual isolation than I might otherwise have been: I was used to living in the world of my own fantasy. But I was timid too, frightened of asserting myself or upsetting my parents, with whom I always felt a close emotional bond. And I think for some time I indulged

another fantasy, without really believing in it, that I might turn out not to be gay after all. It took me quite a while to accept unequivocally that I was.

Was it easy to come out to your parents?
Well, I never really did it. I sort of seeped out, in a muddle of kindliness and cowardice, which of course was unfair to them: I somehow expected them to intuit all sorts of things they hadn't been told. I didn't come out properly until my third year at Oxford. I stayed on there as a graduate student, and chose to write my M.Litt thesis about gay writers who hadn't been able to write openly about their sexuality, particularly E. M. Forster and Ronald Firbank. And that did some of the work of coming out for me, as it were.

Is that what drew you to those writers?
I think I'd long been quite interested by Forster as a gay writer, by what could and what couldn't be said at various times, and what one might be able to say now. You had to bear in mind the culture, the constraints that such writers were working under. It was quite paradoxical really. Forster was working in the tradition of English social comedy but with no real interest in the boy-meets-girl subject which is at that tradition's heart; so he found himself constructing very original variants on it and deviations from it, in which a whole range of gay feelings plays an important if undeclared part. So you could say that the element of self-repression actually bore interesting creative fruit. Firbank too. He invented a completely new and extraordinary, fragmentary, almost nonsensical way of writing as a means of both disguising and expressing the inadmissible things he was longing to say. The equation is often a complicated one between suppression and creativity. A fascinating test-case, I suppose, is Forster's *Maurice*, a novel quite openly about

a gay man, written in 1914, but unpublished in Forster's long lifetime. I think it's a very interesting and touching book in a lot of ways, but it's really nothing like as good a work of art, or as clear-sighted as social commentary, as his novels published in his lifetime.

So I was interested in what happened with and without constraints, especially since I was living in a world where these legal and social constraints had been removed. And I think that was one of the things that fed straight into my first book, *The Swimming-Pool Library*: the idea of contrasting the life of a young person living thoughtlessly and freely in the present, with the life of someone who had grown up under constraints and prohibition.

What about your writing before that?
As an adolescent I had written poetry incessantly, though it later petered out. But I had also always been trying to write fiction, and never finished anything. When I was a graduate student at Oxford, I tried to write an experimental gay novel, but didn't get very far. I haven't looked at it for 25 years, but I suspect there was too much unmediated personal fantasy in it. Later I wrote several chapters of a novel set in Venice, which had a kind of deflected sexual anomaly in it, about a young man who has an affair with his father's mistress. More and more, though, I was struck by the fact that actually I already had an amazingly interesting subject just waiting to be written about in a straightforward way, which had hardly been touched on at all in serious writing.

You have spoken about your writing as beginning from a presumption of the gayness of the narrative position. Given the time when
The Swimming-Pool Library *was published in 1988, was this idea of taking gay subjectivity for granted a bold move on your part?*
It felt to me like a good idea; if you're a writer you have them and you know, and even if they don't necessarily produce good

books, there's a kind of conviction that carries you through. Of course there was other gay fiction: Gay Men's Press published a lot of it, much of it not terribly distinguished; but I don't think there was anyone making a significant impact on the public awareness. In the States there was more, I think. Edmund White's *A Boy's Own Story* came out in 1982, and I wrote what I now see was a rather priggish review of it in the *TLS*. I think I was probably taken aback by its honesty; I'm sure it was still working its effect in my mind when I was starting to write my book two years later.

White stopped short of descriptions of male desire?
Well, there's a bit of brisk buggery in the first chapter, which makes you think that this is how it's going to be, but in fact that's all the sex there is in the whole book. Edmund has later been a pioneer of candour in writing about gay sex, but the strength of that book was its emotional honesty about what for literature was a whole new area of experience: what it was like to be a lost, confused but very sexually driven young gay man growing up in the Midwest, a person who was a complex individual and not a type, however much his experience may have resonated with others. And, as well as its obvious emotional veracity, the book was very highly wrought – perhaps a bit overwrought, some of it – and stylistically self-aware. And that combination was interesting. I may be wrong, but I don't think there was anything like that in British writing.

Was there anything about that particular historical moment that motivated you to write as you did?
The Swimming-Pool Library was more about gay issues perhaps than anything else I have written since, and opens up little windows into earlier gay history. The 1980s was a very ghastly

time. I started writing before the AIDS crisis had really made its impact. While I was writing, the world I was writing about was being changed by this terrible thing, and I had to decide whether or not to make the book itself reflect those changes. After much thought, I decided that it wouldn't. It is set in 1983, and doesn't allude in any direct way to what happened later. But of course it took on all kinds of ironies because of what subsequently occurred. When it came out in 1988 it was, as it were, historical, in a way I couldn't have anticipated when I started writing.

But also there was something about the atmosphere of the mid-1980s, and the anti-gay feelings given grotesque licence by the AIDS crisis, which made writing about gay sex unapologetically and defiantly seem all the more important to me. There were some gay readers who thought it was irresponsible to write about men having unprotected sex with each other, as if people ran away and did automatically what they had read in a novel. People in the grip of an idea are often very unsophisticated readers of fiction. I don't think of it as being in any conventional sense a political book, and its narrator is by design the least political person imaginable; but if there was something novel about the angle the book was written from, then perhaps it did have some sort of political impact. It's really impossible for me to say.

What are the characteristics, though, that mark out a gay narrative position as opposed to a non-gay one – apart from the sexual explicitness?
Well, that book, and my second book, *The Folding Star*, were both written in the first person, so they were written in the persona of a gay man who was writing about his own life. Of course, these are questions that one could tease out endlessly, about whether there are things that are indigenously gay – the way a gay person writes or perceives. Since the novel has dealt overwhelmingly

with heterosexual experience and desire, the fresh angle of the gay narrator has its own logic and value. And I think that was something people weren't used to seeing, because identifiable gay figures in fiction, comic or tragic, had tended to be marginal. They weren't ordinary people whose lives were as complicated and as worthy of interest as anyone else's. I suppose it was that double focus, of gay lives being both ordinary and extraordinary at once, that interested and delighted me.

I'm struck by the emphasis on role playing in your work. Is that emphasis on performance connected with gayness?
That's a difficult question to answer. In *The Line of Beauty*, part of the point is that the world of the novel is permeated with deceit. It's set in a period, the mid-1980s, in which there was a sense of new possibilities, that people might be able to reinvent themselves. Nick himself, for all his social advances, is always half in disguise. I suppose he is someone who has the fantasy that he can live a joined-up life as a gay man in a particular social world that he is drawn to by other kinds of fantasy. He learns in the end that he can't, but I was interested in sustaining a mood of ambiguity, in which we never quite know what Nick and his rather grand straight hosts think of each other. And perhaps, indeed, they don't know either. I think those conditions of emotional uncertainty and half-truths were forced on gay people a lot more then than they are now. I don't think you could write a comparable story set in the present. Things have changed so enormously in the last 20 years.

Pursuit of pleasure features heavily in your work. Is this something gay men in particular are good at?
It's something they're keen on, though they're not invariably good at it. The ability to play outside conventional structures of

love and marriage in the pursuit of pleasure is often envied by straight people. I've always been interested in writing about pleasure seeking. Of course there are many definitions of pleasure, but I suppose we are talking about sexual hedonism.

What about Ecstasy?
Until I was 40 I think I'd always been very ignorant about drug taking, and was generally anxious and disapproving. I dutifully smoked a few joints when I was an undergraduate, but never enjoyed it much, and that was it. I see now that by my late thirties I'd become very withdrawn from the world, and out of touch with what interested and moved younger people. And then I had one of those great happy changes in my life, a big social shift. I was really taken out of myself by someone that I met and fell in love with, and I started hanging out with people who were ten or fifteen years younger than me, and of course I found the world that they – and I – were living in, very interesting and exciting. Taking Ecstasy was part of the mood of that time, and I tried to convey something of its excitement and romance in *The Spell*.

Did you have many gay friends at the time of coming out?
In my later years at Oxford, I had some very important, close gay friends. I think after I had managed to come out, my social world enlarged and opened up in that direction in ways that I couldn't quite allow it to before. But there was clearly a lot more fun to be had when I arrived in London in 1981. One of those Oxford friends was very important to me in taking me around and showing me what could be done, giving me the courage in a way to go into bars and clubs. He was the first person I knew to die of AIDS, in November 1984; indeed, one of the first in this country of whom it was clearly the case. It was especially grim because nobody knew anything about this disease. He and his

family were treated appallingly because of the fear that surrounded it.

What did AIDS do to the underground nature of sexuality?
There was something undeniable about AIDS, though people
sometimes did pretend it was something else, as Rachel pretends
in *The Line of Beauty*, when she claims that her friend picked up
some extraordinary bug in the Far East. But essentially there was
something about it that you couldn't deny. As a consequence,
people were forced to come out. It made people think about gay
sexuality, sometimes initially in a negative way. But in the long
term, if anything good can be said to have come out of it, AIDS
had an educative impact; as well, of course, as serving to politi-
cize gay people.

Do you resist the label 'gay writer'?
I don't resist it, but I don't consider it to be entirely adequate. It's
certainly not a comprehensive description of how I think of
myself as a writer.

What was the general reception of The Swimming-Pool Library?
From a literary point of view, I seem to remember it was generally
a favourable one, though one or two reviewers were frankly
revolted by it, and others took more complicated squirming positions, including an almost anthropological attitude to it, as a book
that you could learn from, if you wanted to, about a strange
category of human behaviour. It was also caught up in the debate
about Clause 28 of the Local Government Bill, and the possibility
that this could lead to the banning of gay fiction from public
libraries.

The success of The Line of Beauty *has been enormous, and has
inevitably put you under the spotlight in a way you weren't before.
There was a predictable reaction from certain parts of the media.
How did you feel about that?*

I didn't expect anything better, so I wasn't shocked or disappointed by it. There were two separate phases of reaction, the first
when the book came out, when it had generally the most
favourable reception of my four books. And then there was a
second wave when it won the Booker, after which it attracted a
different kind of attention. It was written about as the winner of a
prize; and it was noteworthy, I suppose, that a book written from
a gay point of view had won it.

*I was thinking of Chris Smith's comments as the chairman of the Booker
judges, almost removing the gay subject matter as a factor at all.*

Well, I felt that the judges must at least have touched on it in their
meetings. But I think he was simply taking a principled position
and saying that the decision they had reached was not related to
sexual politics.

*Did the fact that the book won indicate a change in attitudes to
homosexuality?*

Yes, I think it did. I had been shortlisted for the Booker ten years
earlier, for *The Folding Star*, and didn't win then; but that could
have been for any number of reasons. Whether its gay aspects
were something that made it difficult for the judges to give it the
prize, we'll never know. I think the relative success of *The Line of
Beauty* is probably an indicator of the big change in attitudes since
1994, though I would also note that the book has sold less well in
paperback so far than any other Booker winner of the past seven
years.

Do you think of the four books you have written since the 1980s in any way as a kind of a completion of a journey, in terms of a project of writing into history a gay history?

To me they have some kind of coherence or unity about them, but that may be just because I wrote them. They certainly weren't conceived at any stage as a project with the purpose of elucidating gay lives. Each book arose of its own imaginative worries and quite personal preoccupations of mine: it's always a fairly mysterious and inward process. I have never set out to represent gay experience in any comprehensive or even particularly responsible way. It's just been my material, if you like, which I have dealt with in my own fashion.

What do you have to say about reports that Andrew Davies has removed the gay sex from his BBC TV adaptation of The Line of Beauty?

They're completely unfair. He has written in two gay sex scenes that aren't in the original. Of course I can see that, to a vigorously heterosexual man like Andrew, the adaptation of a gay novel is a different kind of emotional experience from working on a straight story or a lesbian story, but his concern all along has been in conveying the interest and particularity of the gay characters' lives. It's entirely because of his keen personal desire to adapt the novel that it's being done.

What do you think are the implications of the change in the law in terms of gay partnerships?

I'm reluctant to speak well of this government, but I have to say that its record on gay matters is really a good one. Anything which gives substance and affirmation to the idea of two people of the same sex living together, committing their lives to each other and so on, must be an extremely positive one.

Do you think of yourself as in any way politicized by your experiences as a gay man?
I've never been a politically active person. And I have frequently felt guilty about that. I'm not a joiner, and I slightly dread what happens to people when they get caught up in political life. But I have a strong sense of having, in many ways, ridden on the hard work and struggle of a lot of people who were more committed and clear-sighted than I ever was. At a more general level, there is certainly something about growing up gay (more, perhaps, at the time when I was growing up than now), which forces you to think your own way through many social and moral issues. It's one of the things Forster says in *Maurice*, that being gay has saved Maurice. It stirs and transforms his moral nature, and turns someone who would otherwise have been unthinkingly conventional into a critic of society. You could say that it was the source of a deep and subtle and personal politicization.

Credit: Scott Nunn

Rashida X

In many ways the experience of lesbian, gay, bisexual and trans Muslims today is a throwback to another era. While there now exist civil partnerships, gay adoption, gay clergy and the like in modern British society, the world of British gay Muslims could not be further removed. It's a strange world-within-a-world place in which to exist, but that's what most queer Muslims have to do. It's simply a matter of needs must and getting on with it – which are, funnily enough, very English virtues.

Gay Muslims as a discernible community are a recent phenomenon. Our history to date goes back less than ten years. There were whispers of a gay Muslim group set up by a group of Iranian students that existed in the UK in the 1970s. Rumour had it that they were promptly executed upon their return to Iran. So, as one would imagine, it was with some trepidation that in 1998 we embarked upon setting up Al Fatiha UK (as Imaan was then known).

In September of that year, a group of us were brought together in London by an advert placed in the *Pink Paper* by Faisal Alam, the visiting founder of the Al Fatiha Foundation, the American gay Muslim group. Back then, Muslims who were gay were not part of an identifiable group. If anything, we were part of a larger, mostly London-based Asian presence that congregated at gay Bhangra clubs like Club Kali and Shakti – if at all.

The need to reconcile Islam with homosexuality seemed to coincide with a coming-of-age of my generation of British-born gay Muslims who had witnessed the explosion of gay culture in the larger English cities. It was inevitable that at some point we would start to wonder about our own place within gay culture and the feasibility of reconciling faith and sexuality. This would naturally present several problems. Islam, we were brought up to believe, was wholly against homosexuality. In fact, the gay community as an entity was not even acknowledged, only their practices. I felt then – as I do now – that there was something seriously wrong in this perception. Now my adult self sees that this is a very demeaning way to look at people. It is debasing to us as humans to be judged purely by what we do (and there are some strange ideas about that out there) rather than who we are.

Of course, the assumption was that only men indulged in these practices. Who would have thought Queen Victoria and our parents would have something in common? And white men at that – a *clear* indication of their 'moral inferiority'. Furthermore, we were informed, you could not be gay and Muslim. The two identities were utterly incompatible, an oxymoron, the slimmest hint of the thought was never – nor ever could be – entertained.

This made homosexuality very exciting to me as a teenager! Although I had no inclination of my own queerness until years later, I was fascinated with different lifestyles; probably because my own life seemed at that stage so rigidly laid out before me. It was a given that I, like every other Asian girl I knew, would (God-this-makes-me-puke-to-say-it-now-so-I'll-say-it-quickly) have an arranged marriage. I, however, had other ideas. I wanted to be an artist or a musician. The two appeared to be poles apart, which seems really strange to me now. Don't artists and musicians marry? Anyway, I can't begin to describe how much of a distant fantasy this was to someone like me back then.

I should say here that my sexuality was not a reaction against a restrictive upbringing. There were hundreds of Asian girls at my school who had similar and even more constrained upbringings than mine, and who are vigorously heterosexual today. My parents were immigrants from Pakistan who came to the East End of London in the mid-1960s. Like thousands of others, they flocked to areas where Asian families were already established. Safety in numbers was part of it, but there was also a need to preserve the culture, which was then, as it is now, enmeshed in a rather narrow interpretation of religion. It was an interpretation that did not question or challenge religious orthodoxy, for this would be deemed at best unnecessary and at worst blasphemous.

There are contradictions with Islam in this attitude. Islam teaches Muslims to 'seek knowledge even if it takes you to China'. The possibilities and implications of this were lost on my parents' generation. But one cannot lay blame here. Our parents were busy establishing themselves economically and socially in a country that was far from hospitable to immigrants from the former colonies. Education was a luxury they could not afford – for themselves at least.

Attitudes had not changed much by the late 1990s and in fact they had been cemented by the next generation. It was in these circumstances that the British gay Muslim movement was born.

The new group was named Al Fatiha after the American group. Al Fatiha is the name of the opening chapter in the Quran and was adopted to signify the beginning of a new era. The birth of Al Fatiha UK was an exciting and invigorating affair. Very quickly, plans were made for the very first LGBT Muslim conference. All of us involved in running the group, a collective of about six lesbian and gay Muslims of Pakistani origin, rallied round and began fundraising for the groundbreaking event. We held events in our homes, pulled together resources, called in favours, got people to work for free and eventually we managed to pull together a three-day event.

The day before the conference began, however, disaster struck. Somehow news of the conference was leaked to the press. An article appeared in an Arabic newspaper with details about the event and a reaction from an ultra-conservative Islamic group who had vowed to track the venue down and throw bricks through the windows.

Not wanting to alarm our nervous delegates or the other organizers, we senior organizers decided to keep the information from them to avoid scaremongering and instead inform the authorities. They in turn decided that the most prudent option would be to deploy 40 riot police. So we had an almost comical situation where delegates were happily tucking into tea and biscuits and enjoying the conference while the two of us stood obscuring the view from the window of a small army down below.

Since then we have held three conferences in London and taken part in gay Muslim conferences all over the US. As the UK group evolved and came of age, our name changed to Imaan, meaning 'Faith'. We felt it was important to distinguish ourselves from the Americans because as British Muslims we had our own distinct history and issues.

After years in the shadows of Al Fatiha/Imaan, I suddenly found myself in the position of Chairperson. I had never wanted to be in charge, I didn't want that much responsibility. I was happy enough, of course, to tell everyone what to do and how I thought things should be done – backseat driving, as it were. But suddenly we were without a Chairperson and there didn't seem anyone more suited to fill the role. So I half-reluctantly stepped up.

Today, I treat Imaan as though it were my paid job, but the fact is that I do it for free and in my own time (and sometimes in my bosses' time). Now, I'm considered to be very good at running Imaan, just as I am considered to be very good at my paid job, which has been my career for ten years. Yet the opportunities I have had through Imaan have been far greater than at my paid job. And my professional growth through Imaan has far exceeded it too.

I know there are all kinds of innocent reasons for this, but I think working for Imaan is probably the only job in the world where my sexuality, gender, race and culture are all advantageous and have propelled me forward.

I don't resent working for Imaan for free (though being paid would be nice, funders take note); indeed, I have had so many valuable experiences, met so many amazing people and been to so many places through Imaan that I can hardly complain.

Imaan has had a huge impact on my life. Since becoming Chairperson, I have gained a lot of skills and learnt a lot about managing people and resources, about public relations and about establishing a direction in which to go. I'm lucky in that I am passionate about LGBT Muslim issues and that I have been involved for such a long time. I am so sure in my mind and my heart about our group, our rights and freedoms, and that's what gives me the drive to keep going and make our group stronger and more visible. In short, I have found leadership skills – and that's something I would never have seen in myself before.

It has had a knock-on effect in other areas of work. I have more confidence and believe in my abilities and myself more. But my paid work is totally separate from Imaan, so I can't claim any direct benefit to being gay there. Interestingly enough, however, I am starting to get approached to write more on the subject. There are so few of us who know about Islam and homosexuality, LGBT Muslim issues and the history of the community, that increasingly the press and publishers (as is the case with this book) ask me to submit articles, essays and give interviews and so on. Another thing that's starting to happen more and more is getting asked to organize conferences and lectures, and to speak at festivals and other events. Sometimes I think I could make a career out of it.

These are fascinating times to be gay and Muslim. We have grown in visibility through publicity and media coverage and are highly regarded and called upon for advice by many influential organizations. In 2005 we addressed an audience of 10,000 at Trafalgar Square for London Pride. There is a handful of documentaries and films in production about gay Muslims that feature us; and individuals continually stumble across our website and pour their hearts out to us, shocked that we even exist.

Yet still we cannot openly promote ourselves, it is still too dangerous. There is a menacing rise in bigotry disguised as Islam that we need to protect both ourselves and our members from. At the same time, a surprising development has been the rise of Islamophobia in the gay community. In recent months, Imaan has been embroiled in arguments over Islamophobia with the likes of Outrage, the Lesbian and Gay Christian Movement and the Gay and Lesbian Humanist Association. And we are continually irked by the Muslim-hating bigotry spouted in the web forums of Gay.com and the like.

The constant balancing act of explaining to people about your identity as a gay Muslim can be stressful. People look at you pityingly. It's infuriating. After all, we choose to live this balancing act. We could choose to leave our cultures and faiths and immerse ourselves into gay culture completely. But would we really want to? What is gay culture? We know how gay culture is advertised and promoted in clubs, magazines and on the scene. But scratch beneath the surface and there is little else there. And at the moment it certainly isn't very diverse.

On the positive side, being involved with the gay Muslim community has introduced me to many friends around the world. As someone who has a typically British reserve when meeting new people, I am quite astounded at these new and ever-deepening relationships. At present I am involved in forming an online Muslim lesbian community with the women I met at a recent Al Fatiha conference in Atlanta.

The gay Muslim community is in its infancy, but we are making huge strides, breaking taboos and reaching out to many people who need our support. It can quite literally be a matter of life or death for many people.

Muslims believe in fate. I believe it was my fate to be a part of the gay Muslim movement. I am proud and honoured to have a part in its history.

Credit: Deborah Quenet

Damon Galgut

I have a horror of weddings. This feeling goes back to my early childhood, when the first wedding I attended evoked a sensation in me of being an outcast: somebody standing beyond the circumference of the great wheel of life, watching that vast motion from outside. The sensation was one of exile, inseparable in my mind from powerlessness.

South Africa in those days was a conservative, oppressive place, and to be gay was a crime. Times have changed, obviously, and we now have one of the most famously liberal constitutions in the world. It is not quite law yet, but it is surely only a matter of legal formalities before gay marriage is possible here. At least on paper, gay people enjoy near-equal rights with other citizens.

In theory, then, my life should have changed dramatically. All kinds of things are possible for me that were not possible when I was growing up. But in fact my life is more constricted, less connected to the mainstream, than it was ten years ago. This is a matter of choice: I cling to my outsider position these days as if it is a source of power that should be defended at all costs. And indeed, if I am honest about it, that is exactly what I believe it to be.

*   *   *

South Africa's bad old days were made only partly of politics. Or rather: the politics were possible because of a system of beliefs and values that seemed to be fixed in place, like some eternal truth. At the top of the pyramid of power was the white man, and the world was made in his image.

If you had no reason to doubt this version of things, you would simply take up your appointed place. And my place was not bad. Quite the opposite: without any effort on my part, I could have followed in the footsteps of my father, and of his father before him, into wealth and privilege and comfort, with all the less fortunate below me.

And in a certain sense, of course, I did follow that expected path. Not for me the bitter road into exile or armed resistance; my nature did not allow for that kind of courage. My rebellion was internal and invisible and, on a practical level, quite useless. It was a refusal to accept the order around me as natural. That kind of doubt – though it may begin with politics – very rapidly starts to undo all the values and beliefs around you. Or rather, it makes you wonder at the reasons why people believe and act the way they do.

So the fact that I did not slip mindlessly into power was not due, alas, to my superior conscience. It was because of my sexuality. That feeling I had as a guest at the wedding was a reflection of my position in South African life generally: of being outside the circle of power, looking in. It was a position that I shared, of course, with all the other lesser beings who had been excluded, but in my case it was unnatural. Women and black people were *meant* to be excluded; I was an impostor, a betrayer. Only I knew it in those days, but I would be found out in time.

For a long time I maintained the lie, the false face, keeping my loneliness a secret. I hated my peers, even as I imitated them, the white boys slowly turning into white men, who had never doubted themselves. Not only in politics, but in their personal and social lives too. They were, by definition, right about everything, while I was riddled with doubt. I wanted desperately to be like them, to be ignorant and unreflective and content.

Of course it happened as I feared: the lie was too weak to stand up, and in the end I was found out. If I'd imagined that the truth would be redeeming, it didn't happen like that; the doubt only amplified and grew. But gradually, as the years and years of being 'other' piled up, my sense of myself began to change.

There was no big, definitive moment when I saw the light; but one day, very quietly, I reached the point where I didn't *want* to be like these other white men any more. Their confidence and superiority, which had once been so intimidating, now looked like arrogance. Their assumptions about the world, and about themselves, which I had envied and admired, were repellent. And my distance and difference from them, which had felt like power-lessness, began to feel like a kind of power.

*   *   *

It is a power I am reluctant to give up. Even now, or perhaps especially now. The temptation is to leap in and belong; to join all the other gay people who are celebrating and taking part, and contemplating the prospect of marriage. But if I am truthful, the idea of being in such a community fills me with horror.

The reason has to do with temperament – I have never been one for parades and parties – but also with mistrust. I have learned, from my years of inner exile, that to belong to a group of people, any group at all, is to share in its beliefs and assumptions. Perhaps not unquestioningly, but to a degree where self-knowledge is blunted. A certain sentiment grows up around groups, and sentiment is nearly always untruthful. There is solidarity and support in such belonging, of course, which is a form of power in itself. And there is no reason to believe that the South African gay community is about to inflict any kind of oppression on anybody. But I feel safer and stronger – more in possession of objective knowledge – if I am outside the circle, looking in.

To be solitary, to refuse one's internal loyalty to other people: of what use is that to anybody? None – except, perhaps, to a writer. If I did any other kind of work, I might see the virtues of allegiance. There are, of course – there always have been – many gay writers who feel differently from me. One thinks of Proust or Tennessee Williams or Patrick White, for example – all writers who have, as it were, burrowed *into* their identity, mining it for characters and themes that are outside the range of most straight men. However secretive and self-loathing, a certain sense of belonging is needed for such a project.

But one can go in the other direction, and that is the way I have chosen. I have cultivated dispassion and distance. Like the writers I have mentioned, my literary sensibility is inseparable from my sexuality, but not in a warm, inclusive sense. As with many gay people, alienation was an early trauma – until I fell in love with alienation. As a writer and as a human being, I have paid a price for this. Leaving aside the personal, I select a literary example: it's expected of gay writers either that they create spectacularly convincing female characters, or that they have no understanding of women at all. Having no ambition to do the first, I have been accused of the second. But of course it isn't true: what I have done is to turn the same cold eye on women that I use on men, and to look at their relative positions of power in the same way. The picture that emerges is hardly ever consoling or pleasant.

Is it the duty of writers to celebrate their humanity, or to look at it critically, from a distance? Well, there are already people who do the first task very well – far better than I ever could. The second requires powers that most writers avoid, probably sensibly. But they are the powers, however small, that my sexuality has given me, and to which I have committed myself.

So I cannot tell you very much about the way we are now. That things have changed is obvious. But for me, not a lot is different. I am a gay man, and that fact has shaped almost every aspect of my being. But I have no gay lifestyle to speak of, none of the trappings and indulgences that give a feeling of belonging. Being white and male, but gay: the armour of power, turned inside out, is a strange suit of clothes indeed. Through the wrong end of a telescope, through concentric circles of alienation, the world comes into a different sort of focus. It is, very often, a peculiar world – but then what seems normal and acceptable is usually peculiar, if one is not connected to it.

Credit: Gerry Lane

Robert Taylor

I joined the Royal Air Force in 1975. I was $16^{1}/_{2}$. Back in the 1970s homosexuality in the armed forces was illegal. I was fully aware that I was gay, and determined to remain completely closeted. Homophobia generally, and particularly in military circles, was so normal that it did not occur to me that I could live openly as a gay man, have gay sex or form a normal loving relationship. But it was not an altogether sensually barren existence. I remember feelings of surprise and amused guilt at the pleasure I derived from the attentions of a very 'thorough' male doctor during my initial RAF medical. There was also a lot of warm affectionate male bonding going on with even the most macho of my colleagues.

Forces life was surprisingly unproblematic from the gay point of view. Being 6 foot 2 inches, black, and very fit was a great 'beard'! It was just assumed that I was some kind of urban stud, albeit with a rather unlikely RP accent. I did not really notice at the time but, looking back it seems that most of my best mates were other similarly sensitive young men, untroubled by the attentions of women. Nobody was even *remotely* 'out' or even ambiguous about their sexuality. It was just too dangerous.

My gay life began in 1977 during a long leave in Birmingham. I went to a CHE (Campaign for Homosexual Equality) social centre one evening, declared my sexuality and my strong desire to 'do something about it'. I remember a long, gentle conversation with a very kind and rather gorgeous counsellor. He would have been the perfect person to start practising with, but he was thoroughly professional and probably quite used to handling such yearnings. I did not have to wait too long for some expression. Within three weeks I had met the man I was to be with for the next 14 years. I am clear that meeting that man was one of the luckiest and most critical moments of my life.

While still serving in the RAF my gay life amounted to two heady days per fortnight in Birmingham, 90 miles away from my RAF station, with my secret boyfriend and a small circle of new gay friends. The secrecy and danger made this new bit of my identity all the more precious, and my big butch work identity all the more absurd. At work I was someone completely different: seemingly single but mysteriously more happy and fulfilled than most of the people around me.

I was very good at my job, but having experienced a bit of fun self-expression, wanted much more. I left the RAF at 20, not having been outed, and very keen to explore the possibilities of living fully as myself.

I did a law degree, qualified as a barrister and was then imme-diately head-hunted for a job in educational publishing which became more and more photography related. I took up photogra-phy full time in 1989.

The Law as a career had never really been a serious option. I had done well at university and drifted a little further in that direction merely because it seemed sound and looked good. Lawyers also struck me as a rather traditional lot, and after the forces I was not interested in anything that would be too person-ally restrictive. In my publishing job I was working for a gay man in a mixed but relatively liberal environment. Moving on from that to working as a freelance photographer whose images had such a lot of gay content took me right to the other end of the spectrum of self-expression. Suddenly I was – in many work-related ways – more expressed as a gay man than most gay people I knew.

These days I do less specifically gay-related work, but many, if not most, of my clients know or quickly work out that I am gay. For most people the bigger news seems to be that I am black. I've found that if they can handle my race, my sexuality is usually just another flavour.

Legally and politically much has changed for the better. I enjoy a very real sense of increased personal freedom to be myself as a direct result of society's growing acceptance of queer folk and same-sex relationships. I really appreciate the progress, particularly when I reflect on the reminiscences of my friends in their sixties, seventies and eighties. I'm also clear that some of the biggest barriers to my personal and professional progress over the years have been as much self-inflicted as imposed from outside. My professional progress as an out gay man has been marked as much by taking the courage to liberate myself in my work as by gaining 'acceptance' from anyone else.

Back in the early 1990s I was a lot more cautious than I needed to be. It was fine being a face on the gay scene and in the gay media, but I was still a bit of a closet case when it came to the mainstream. These days, I notice – particularly when I'm out and about with younger gay friends – that I'm still more cautious about public displays of affection than they are. This is partly a hangover from my time in the RAF when it really *was* dangerous to be identified as gay. It may also be a little to do with the fact that many of my gay friends are white, making our public relatedness that bit more conspicuous than it might be if we were of the same race.

I'm wary of assuming that mainstream views about homosexuality have changed very much beyond surface pieties and PC 'scripts' though. If things have moved on so much, why are most young men still so terrified that they might be thought gay? I don't think I come across as particularly predatory, but even the coolest heterosexual men that I meet seem to need to make sure that it's understood which way they swing, once they learn that I am gay.

I'm proud of the fact that although I am relatively socially cautious, my photographic work is not (see www.taylor-photo. co.uk). It has always featured lots of nudity and pro-gay content that seems to have been valued as a positive and intelligent contribution to the gay community as well as curious thoughtful heterosexuals.

My career was just getting started as the gay community was getting better organized in its response to HIV/AIDS. During the early 1990s there was a great drive to reclaim the right to enjoy our sexuality at a time when some elements of the mainstream were trying to drive us back into a celibate closet. Some – particularly the religious lobby – even tried to claim that this was for our own good, but the hostility and contempt for us and our 'nature' was rather ill-concealed.

Suddenly good sex education had become a matter of life and death. Sexually active gay men needed good, well-presented information that did *not* make safer sex seem so dull that they might not think it worth bothering with. As a photographer with a reputation for work with a strong erotic element, I was much in demand for illustrating all sorts of safer-sex campaigns. My biggest and most outrageous splash was probably a full-colour safer-sex education book produced with Peter Tatchell called *Safer Sexy* (Cassell, 1994). At a time of growing censorship, the book featured extensive full-colour photography showing literally everything that its thorough and explicit text described. We got away with 'murder' in the name of vital health education. I remember *Boyz* magazine doing an erection count and concluding that it was probably hotter than anything else you could buy legally at the time. Yet as it was widely accepted as serious high-quality sex education material you could go and pick up a copy (shrink-wrapped of course!) in W. H. Smith and Waterstone's, as well as the more predictable specialist outlets.

In addition to the specifically gay health education opportunities coming my way, I also benefited greatly from being part of an almost exclusively gay network that provided lots of openings for my photography – by no means all gay-related in their content. I even made my first sales of work to the National Portrait Gallery via an informal gay social connection, and there are countless other breaks that came my way via predominantly gay contacts.

For a period near the beginning of my career a lot of my most successful art photography centred on gentle abstract explorations of issues to do with sexual identity, and to a lesser degree its links with racial and cultural identity. I'm pretty certain there would not have been as much interest if my work had centred on heterosexuals' experiences!

So yes, being gay made a big *positive* difference to my professional life.

On the negative side, there may have been some professional doors closed to me – as much because of my race as my sexual orientation – but I'm not too aware of them. My gay contacts seem to feature much less in sourcing work opportunities these days.

I find it difficult to determine the specific degree to which my gayness may be affecting the course and quality of my current professional or personal life: there are so many possible explanations for the way things have turned out. In any event, I'm more aware of privilege and lucky breaks than hardship or hurdles.

Then again, it depends on the subtlety with which one analyses these things. While I have not suffered any really crude abuse or outright resistance to my presence anywhere as a gay man, self-censorship and low expectations tend to cloud the view. For me, the issues arising on the street and in the commercial world are relatively straightforward compared to those that crop up around the conduct of family life, committed relationships and developing a healthy self-respecting gay community.

The extent to which things have progressed seems far *less* clear to me when I reflect on the finer and more intimate aspects of feeling free or encouraged to lead a *full* life as a gay man. It's great that soon I will be able to have nearly all the rights that heterosexuals enjoy if I go ahead with plans to formalize my relationship with the man I have loved for the last 11 years. But I only have to think about some of the issues that emerge when I really confront the practicalities and consequences of 'marrying' my partner to see that I have a long way to go to feel truly liberated. There are still lots of people in my life that I'd think twice about sharing this great news with, despite the fact that I'm supposed to be so 'out'. What difference would it make to our lives if our union became 'official'? At the moment we still enjoy a certain degree of very welcome privacy and control over our social profile. Who would we want to tell? Who would we include in the celebrations? How many supposedly cool heterosexuals would have issues about taking our same-sex union as seriously as their own intimate relationships?

As a community we should definitely be fighting for something of equal value. I think I'd be happier if it was nonetheless different enough to reflect our arguably different needs, priorities and interests.

As a gay man, my personal sense of being able to enjoy full human rights and dignity is definitely compromised. There are still members of my immediate family and people I encounter in routine social situations who are openly and vigorously hostile to the idea of same-sex relationships having as full a range of rights as those taken for granted by heterosexuals. It bothers me that such bigotry and intolerance are still so prevalent, acceptable and able to *still* have such an impact on so many people's freedom to be themselves. I think particularly of very young vulnerable people for whom sexuality and identity are complicated enough in themselves without having to deal with a hostile environment. The law may be moving forward – and I'm very grateful – but in the family, the school playground and in a host of environments where real life is lived out in a fairly casual unstructured way, homophobia is still rife, impacting on people's lives quite negatively.

Additionally, gauging the extent to which homophobia may have impacted on the exercise of my human rights and my full dignity as a human being is complicated by my being black, and to a lesser extent, coming from a working-class background.

Overall I'd say that I'm one of the lucky ones for whom being different has drawn largely positive and supportive attention. Sadly, I don't feel that I'm so typical.

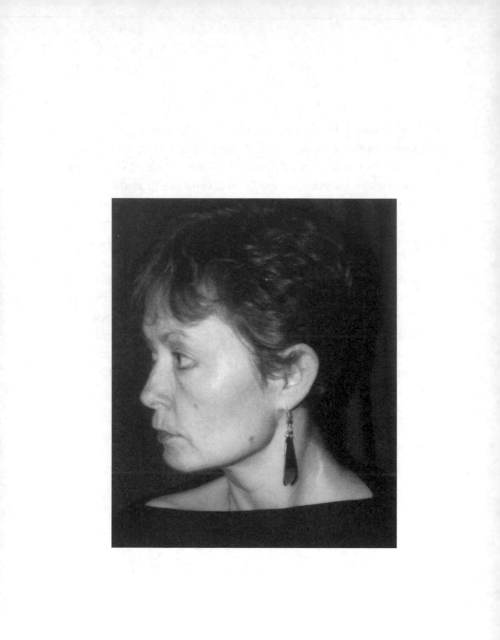

V. G. Lee

Here goes! I'm 56. Tall with short, blonde hair. I wear glasses. Enjoy gardening. Own house, no car, non-smoker, GSOH. I live alone with two cats for company. I consider myself the stereotypical middle-aged single lesbian as opposed to the stereotypical middle-aged, one half of a lesbian couple, but who knows what the future holds? Straight people want to know if I'm lonely. Do I find as I get older that I have fewer friends, that there are fewer places to go, fewer things to do?

'NO!' I tell them, 'On the contrary. Incredibly, even to me, life has got better. More friends. More places to go. More things to do.'

I was 29 when I spotted my first lesbian. The word 'lesbian' probably had never passed my lips up till then. I'd vaguely heard of them but I imagined there were probably only nine or ten in the whole country; disaffected drabs who couldn't bag a bloke. I'd bagged a bloke.

I remember, when I was 16 years old, studying my reflection in the window of Sketchley's Dry Cleaners and thinking, 'Val, you're going to be left on the shelf.' I went home utterly dismal, but then I met Ray who looked like the good-looking one in the Bee Gees, and he liked me. Then he loved me. Me! All lanky five-foot nine with the sticky-out ears that Dad said reminded him of Dumbo the elephant. I wasn't in love but I was so proud to have a boyfriend. And relieved. And grateful. We became known as Ray-and-Val. Once in the early years I had even knitted jumpers for us, in red and black with our names worked into them. If Ray went into the local Tesco's on his own, the manager or the sales-girls would ask, 'Where's Val?' And the same for me. But that was rare because we went everywhere together. It was like we'd entered a tunnel almost immediately after meeting and we tootled along inside that tunnel learning little of the outside world until I went to art college in my late twenties – and spotted my first lesbian. And made my first gay friends, David and Carl.

For four years (in secret) I had a relationship with another woman. I thought of her as being the lesbian and me as the glamorous, unfaithful wife. I was desperate not to lose my straight identity or for anyone to find out. Her life didn't tempt me at all. Nobody where she worked knew she was gay, hardly any of her friends knew, or her family. I thought her life seemed full of possible minefields. At that time I wanted to balance everything, let nothing drop.

So why did I eventually leave Ray, my home and secure suburban life for a tiny airless flat at the top of a Victorian house in Hackney, north London?

I left because when I looked ahead into my future, I couldn't bear to see myself on the same path, doing the same things. I left because I couldn't bear my husband to touch me and treat me as if I was his property, and I was crumbling under the immense strain of living a lie – those unguarded moments when I might forget who I was with.

The day before I left we went to see Bruce Springsteen in concert. I remember Ray crying as Springsteen sang about 'having a house and a girl, having something going for him in this world'. I couldn't allow myself to cry because he'd have seen that as a sign of hope for the two of us. The next morning I just went, taking a bin-bag of clothes and not much more.

This was 20 years ago. I didn't walk straight into a brand-new life. My relationship had broken up six months earlier and my first year alone was one of utter emptiness and dislocation.

Such a drastic measure didn't mean I immediately proclaimed

myself a lesbian. If I had there would have been nobody around to listen. Anyway, I wasn't sure that I wanted to be a lesbian. All my confidence over the years had come out of the straight world, the status I'd felt by being married. Suddenly I realized that I hadn't just cut myself off from a husband, I'd lost his family as well and caused them so much pain. I'd loved his mum more than I'd loved my own mum. I lost our few friends. My own family kept their distance just in case I came to my senses and went back.

I had never been on my own before. We hadn't been a couple who went to pubs and clubs. I'd never even been abroad. At first I was petrified of going anywhere, particularly if it meant getting back to my flat after dark. London frightened me. I might be a grown woman but inside I hadn't moved much further from the despondent teenager standing outside Sketchley's. 'Lesbian', 'gay', 'dyke' – I couldn't bring myself to use those words, certainly not about myself. They made me shudder. They were nothing to do with me. I blurred the issue even to myself. I liked particular, special people of either sex – which didn't mean I was bi-sexual. I shuddered at that title as well. I refused to categorize myself. Not from any fine principle but from fear and shame of what 'people' might think of me.

It took a year to get used to London. N16 may be a lesbian hotspot now but in 1985 it was only just starting to warm up. I had my one friend, Mary, who lived on the other side of London, and finally when I felt confident enough we joined a lesbian group in Willesden. My first memory is a meeting in somebody's front room. I was still clinging on to being able to pass for a straight woman and I wore a full white skirt and matching blouse, both scattered with a pattern of strawberries. Over my shoulder I carried a white patent handbag containing my purse and a lipstick. As I walked into the room I distinctly heard a woman mutter, 'Bloody hell, it's not a garden party.'

In my ignorance I had imagined I'd be welcomed with enthusiasm. *And* in my conceit, because in my previous straight life I'd
been considered attractive. From being a plain child over the
years I'd managed a duckling-to-swan metamorphosis and I
valued it. 'Wow!' was what I'd expected. Appreciative women
jumping up to offer me their seat. Apart from that one remark, I
was ignored. The talk was of tennis and women's football teams.
OK for Mary who played tennis and football but not OK for me.
I'd prided myself on not being a sporty type. They were unattractive and masculine or tomboyish like Mary. Mary could do most
things but then she had known who and what she was since being
a young child – I'd tried to be whatever other people wanted me
to be. I hadn't an original idea of my own, and I still parroted
everything my parents and husband said. Pretty, feminine,
conceal all strength, that was my ideal.

For a few more years I hung on to my blouses and skirts. I
fought change as if my life depended on it – which did me no
good at all. I made no progress and was confused and unhappy.
Mary stoically remained a good friend. She advised counselling
but I resisted that. Why would I need some female vegetarian
with bad dress-sense to explain the best bits of my life away?

I was hostile towards all routes taking me towards assimilating;
and, fair enough, most gay women I met were hostile to me. I
have stood on the perimeter of meetings and felt I was a stranger
in another country where I had no clue to the language being
spoken. I remember I tried to look confident. This made no difference. Looking back, it did seem to me as if the ranks were closed
to women who didn't conform. Nobody had the time or the inclination to pause and think how frightening it was to be lost
between worlds, as I so obviously was. Even now I hear remarks
about married women: 'They're only using you, an affair with a
married woman is a train crash waiting to happen', and yet so

many of the women I meet have been married. Often, extricating themselves has been incredibly painful. Walking away doesn't immediately make life a 'win' situation, there are losses on both sides. How do you leave children behind, how do you take children away from someone they love? I didn't have children, but I left behind my Siamese cat that I'd had for 15 years. This might seem superficial set against uprooting children, but feeling that I had deserted my cat who had been so attached to me, and knowing that the cat went downhill physically almost immediately, was so painful.

As I wrote at the beginning, life did get better. I began going to adult education courses at Hackney College. In the morning I did gardening, afternoons I attended a women-only creative writing class run by Carla, accompanied by her bouncy rescue dog. I found I could write and that going to classes with no expectation of being understood or finding a partner somehow released me to start opening out. No, I wasn't a sporty woman but I was a writing woman. For the first time I was able to look critically at my many prejudices. I see the woman I was and hardly recognize her. I do feel sorry for that Val, and the struggle she made of her life. At the writing class I met similar women, some of whom were sporty as well – as was my first real friend since meeting Mary, Robyn.

I didn't spot Robyn immediately. The first time I saw her she wore a smart, scarlet trouser suit. I was still pretty much entrenched in my stereotypical perceptions. I thought she must be a comfortably-off housewife, children at school and time on her hands. Wrong. Robyn had a career, wrote fiction, staged plays, played tennis, softball, football. Twelve years later and she's running, swimming and biking in triathlons. *And* she can still look great in a chiffon dress and a pair of wings and be the fairy from the top of the Christmas tree!

Robyn asked me to a dinner party and introduced me to two other writers, Helen and Frances, who were both very witty and also made me feel at ease enough in their company to be quite witty myself. These three women remain my good friends to this day.

Writing became my conduit to being accepted and to accepting myself. Over time I was able to let go of my fixed ideas of what constituted an attractive, successful woman. I went out more and this time my attempts to join in weren't met with hostility. I found there was more tolerance for women just being themselves in all their different ways. With two other straight friends, myself and Carla the writing tutor, we formed a cabaret group, All Mouth, No Trousers. We wanted to encourage women to perform; to sing, dance, play a musical instrument, read or recite poetry. Each performance we allowed one male act. The very first event was held in a shop basement on Stoke Newington High Street. It was a runaway success. We multi-tasked: performing, compèring, cooking food, pouring drinks, taking money while having a smashing, exuberant evening. It was the first really exciting event I'd ever taken part in. After that, every three months or so AMNT got together to put on a show.

Which brings me to Millennium year, 2000. Diva Books was launched under the editorship of the fabulous Helen Sandler. In the few years they were publishing regularly they gave many lesbian authors the chance to break through with their writing. They published my first novel, *The Comedienne*, the story of how unlucky-in-love and oddball Joanie Littler found romance and popularity among her peers. A novel put together from my own abysmal attempts to forge relationships and the 'Joanie' stories I had written for the AMNT cabaret nights.

So, did life get better because I had changed, or have our lives improved anyway? Four of us assembled at my kitchen table this morning: Sheila, one-half of a long-term relationship; Mary,

one-half of an erratic relationship; Norma; and myself – two spin-
sters of the parish.

'Have things got better for us?' I challenged.

Furrowed brows all round.

'I'm enjoying my retirement,' Norma says.

'That's not what I mean. Have things got better or worse for us
as lesbians?'

A universal 'Yes!'

'Well, come on, in what way?'

Sheila says, 'As you know, I've got the builders in at the
moment. Twenty years ago I'd have pretended I lived with a
woman friend, no more than that. I'd have been embarrassed and
nervous of them finding out about us and becoming hostile. My
builder calls my girlfriend "The Governor". "What colour paint-
work does 'The Governor' want?" We've met his wife. We've sat
and chatted. I'm not saying I'm grateful for being accepted, but it
wouldn't have happened in the past.'

Everyone wants to get a word in now, we're nodding and
leaning forward across the table. Mary says, 'I've wasted a big
chunk of my life being scared of what my family and friends
would think of me if they knew.' (Mary is 52.) 'My best friend all
through school and since, I only told her I was gay about two
years ago. Only five or six years ago I told my mum and dad. I've
spent years listening to other people telling me about what's
going on in their lives rather than talking about myself.'

'But is it better now?' I persisted.

'Of course it is. I go to dance classes. There are dances at
Jackson's Lane and the Rivoli Ballroom, weekends at Eastbourne,
I don't like driving in the fog . . .'

Norma cuts across this with the observation that she never
even heard the word 'lesbian' until quite late in her development
and, like me, assumed that we were thin on the ground.

'I see women hand in hand all the time down here in Hastings,' Sheila says; 'and nobody blinks an eye.'

'I wouldn't go as far as that, Sheila,' I interject. 'I think people often do blink eyes, but most of them decide to live and let live; however after dark, when they've had a few drinks, I think it could get quite unsafe. Earlier this year a group of gay men travelling on the train from Brighton to Hastings for "Queer on the Pier" had to be protected by the guard from a gang of homophobic youths.'

'Yes, Val,' Mary says, 'but ten years ago, the guard might have been homophobic and left them to get beaten up, and even two years ago there was no "Queer on the Pier" to go to.'

Exit Mary to paint my bathroom ceiling, Sheila and Norma to paint the insides of Sheila's kitchen cupboards, me to the shopping precinct to buy Christmas presents for my nephew, his partner and their two children, who know I'm gay, who buy my books, who come to my readings.

I'll tell you how different life feels now compared to ten, twenty, thirty years ago – which is as far back as I go. It feels as if we're not thousands of small isolated pockets, sometimes just one or two of us to an area, getting on with our neighbours and work colleagues as long as there's a tacit agreement not to make any reference to our sexuality. Yes, there still remain towns and villages where little progress has been made, but now we're like an increasingly complicated and strong cat's cradle – so many, many more strands linking us together.

There *are* more opportunities for finding friends and relationships. A few years ago I moved to Hastings on the south coast, a small town like many others. Within months the Hastings Rainbow Alliance was formed. There is a lesbian book group, supper club, lesbian Yahoo group with over 200 members. There's the aforementioned 'Queer on the Pier', with clubbers being bussed in from Brighton and London, LGBT-friendly pubs and restaurants, and next summer the first Hastings LGBT Arts Festival. I could go out several times a week. If I wanted to hop on a train to Bexhill, Eastbourne or Brighton I could go out every night of the week. Is this upsurge a twenty-first-century phenomenon? Whether by luck or intent, it seems to be.

And I can't finish without mentioning the advent of the York Lesbian Arts Festival. It was launched by Jenny Roberts as the Libertas Lesbian Arts Festival about the same time that Diva Books began publishing and has grown from a humble yet thrilling start to a huge event attracting thousands of women for the two-day Book Festival, concerts and workshops. Seeing the variety of women taking part, being part of the event myself makes me aware of the long journey I've been able to make.

And yes, there's dancing, ballroom and salsa, there are women with camper vans, holiday lets, life coaching, the Gay Games, Pride events, pubs, clubs, bars and knitting circles, tennis, football, handball, golf – I'm stopping now but I could go on and on.

Credit: Dimitris Theocharis

Daniel Harbour

My grandfather had hidden every trace of the affair. Throughout his life, he had simply refused to discuss the matter.

My mother recalls, as a girl, taking down a book in the study and finding a strange man's name inscribed in the cover. 'Dad, who is *Zel-man Kagar-lit-ski*?' she had asked, slowly sounding the name out. My grandfather muttered something poorly improvised and took the book away. ('What did he say?' my partner, Dierk, asked when my mother told us the story earlier this year. 'I don't know. But it wasn't an answer.' 'And the book?' 'We never saw it again. It vanished.') My grandfather was not someone with whom one could push such points. A 'No' was most definitely a 'No'.

His brother-in-law had also tried to broach the subject, without success. Writing to me after my grandfather's death, when the years of secrecy had begun to unravel, he said, 'I can never forgive Emmanuel for lying to Lilian and me.'

It is ironic, given common talk of burying the truth and of bearing secrets to the grave, that it was precisely the shadow of death that cast light on the matter. For, despite his secrecy, my grandfather had destroyed nothing. Several years after his death, we found letters, photographs, diaries, old passports, salvaged newspaper articles. Whole lives, lived before our memories, began to unfold. If he had wanted permanent secrecy, he would surely have destroyed everything. Unless the loss of love was pain enough, not to be compounded by destroying its traces?

And so began the slow process of piecing things together: examining photographs, deciphering the letters' pre-Revolutionary Russian scrawl, translating, dating, retracing journeys across

Europe, scouring antique newspapers for the name or place or topic that had caused them to be kept.

Initially, it was the letters that had aroused suspicion. Sandwiched between prosaic paragraphs about health and shopping and loans and title deeds were passages of fumbling furtiveness: anonymized addresses, transparent 'codes', meetings and activities deliberately unnamed. 'Destroy my letters without fail' ended one, explaining perhaps why only half the correspondence had come down to us: safer to keep one's tracks covered.

But it was my 'cousin' Buckie's discovery of the photograph that probably clinched things: a group of men, well dressed, formally posed, with my great-grandfather off to the left and, just a few places forward, centre-stage, the unmistakable beard and face of Vladimir Ilyich Lenin.

The facts were undeniable. My great-grandparents, who had barely survived the Stalinist purges, were not mere victims of the 1917 Revolution. They had been instigators at its inception.

Of course, hindsight offers unrivalled clarity. It was not until my grandmother's eightieth birthday that everything came together.

No one alive remembers my great-grandparents. They have passed away, and only their children's spouses, who never knew them, survive them; my grandfather and his siblings have passed on too. So, initially, it was a mystery as to why my grandfather had hidden the truth about them away, why he had lied to his sister and brother-in-law about possessing their letters, why he had refused to tell my mother that the name she had found in the book that vanished was her deceased grandfather's.

Of course, everyone had hunches and inklings. He had adored his parents. He had lost his father young. He had left school to be a 14-year-old breadwinner for his mother and siblings. And then his mother too had died. What a terrible fall! She began her life in luxury, the daughter of a major timber merchant with dealings from Moscow to Alexandria, and had ended it poor, if not in poverty – surviving, in part, on the sale of heirlooms. And perhaps bitterest of all to her son was that his success as bread-winner proved to be peerless – a captain of British industry, fêted and knighted – but too late to be any use or pleasure to his beloved mother. So, we surmised, the letters and photographs held too many memories of hardship and loss. Better to keep them and the feelings locked away. They were wounds not to be opened, even by his sister or daughter.

The Communist connection only emerged slowly, as I began to edit the letters over the course of some 18 months. Initially, it was Ludmilla who spotted it. Officially, she is an expert in reading Russian handwriting (her skill has proved invaluable). Unoffi-cially, she is an expert in reading between the lines, that most Russian of arts. I made mental notes of the points she raised, but did not pay too much attention. After all, work on the 'family archive', as it became known, was moonlighting for me and, when I could make time, I concentrated on whatever fragment was before my nose without giving thought to the bigger picture.

Whenever a new translation emerged, I would drop by my grandmother's, have tea, and leave a copy. She would call a while later, full of enthusiasm, thanks, questions. 'These people are coming alive for me,' she remarked several times. 'They've never been more than names on tombstones, and now, finally, they're coming alive. Such idealists. So sophisticated and educated. I wonder what they would have made of the silly girl I was when your grandfather married me . . .' Whichever member of the family was the next to visit – sibling, child, cousin, nephew, niece, grandchild – would be taken into the 'archive room', with its boxes, envelopes, briefcases and concertina files, all hoarding their old secrets, to 'read the latest'.

In this way, news of the project and interest in it began to spread. In due course, I have found myself in correspondence with Scotland, Israel, Russia, Canada and the United States. As my grandmother's eightieth birthday approached, and with relations flying in from four continents, she asked whether I could make a short speech about the archive and our findings.

It was only at this point, as I started to tie together all of the translations, that the big picture began to become clear. I had chosen the letters for translation mostly at random, based on the clarity of the handwriting. Virtually no letter was dated and only a few were in their original, postmarked envelopes. And even so, the postmarks frequently proved to be of limited use. Having been hurriedly and imprecisely placed, they were often only partially legible. On their arrival in Russia, they were postmarked a second time, on the reverse side; but this second date, far from helping, only increased the confusion, as the Russian receipt date seemed to precede the German despatch. For instance, one of my favourite letters – in which my great-grandmother instructs my great-grandfather in the science of obtaining, from Ekaterinoslav merchants, the best in arctic fox boas ('You must choose the *whitest*, otherwise they are sometimes yellowish, which is worthless', 'After the season, 30 rubles', 'Three years ago . . .') – left Germany on 27 November 1912 and reached Russia on 18 November 1912, seemingly nine days before departure.

Eventually, a passing comment in one of the letters, about travelling to Switzerland before a passport expired, resolved the problem: in those days, Russia still followed the Julian calendar and so was 13 days behind Western Europe on the Gregorian calendar. The apparent trip nine days back through time amounted to an efficient transit of four days.

Yet, even with postmarks, fewer than half the letters could be dated directly. So, I now found myself poring over them, comparing the content of the dated ones with that of the undated ones, seeking out small clues. In one case, there was a match between mention of my great-grandmother's Parisian tailor (in a dated letter) with the headed notepaper of the Grands Magasins du Printemps, Paris of another (undated). In another case, there was mention of a registered letter sent from the Black Forest one week earlier; so, I set about searching through all the envelopes to find one marked 'Eingeschrieben'. It eventually emerged, on a heavily smudged, later reused, dark orange envelope.

Working the letters in this way, closely and in tandem, Ludmilla's observations suddenly rang true. Certain phrases did stick out, certain appellations were definitely pseudonyms. Some sentences made more sense if one read 'politics' for 'weather'. A clear example:

I agree with you that all business affairs must be wound up, especially after the case with Umanski. But I hope that the *weather* will settle down and, thus, you will be able to extricate yourself in a couple of weeks.

Sometimes the introduction of code was explicit: 'All you need is *dol*, (I'm afraid to write [*dollars*] fully. I will write "greens".)'

And then there were the congresses and meetings in Bern and Zurich, when the leaders of the 1917 Revolution were plotting in exile. The name Sverdlov even makes an appearance (in the feminine – Sverdlov himself was probably already in Siberia at that stage, dreaming of the Politburo he would one day run). When one took all the small signs and fragments of evidence into account, the case was compelling, even if not conclusive.

A month before my grandmother's birthday, my cousin had her leaving party. She was headed to Canada. A very impressive party, if not a very impressive leaving: she was to be back for the birthday party a month later. As father of the leaver and owner of the venue (his house), my uncle was in attendance. As the party rolled down, he asked what I was planning on saying in my speech at the birthday party. As I generally plan speeches only a few hours before making them, I told him I did not know – at that stage, the Communist themes were only just becoming clear – but that I planned on keeping it short.

'That's fine. I'll look forward to hearing more. We're asking everyone to keep to between four and six minutes. Otherwise all the speeches will drag on.'

Mention of 'everyone' worried me. How many speeches were planned, I wondered; but asked, more tactfully, 'Who is going to be speaking?'

'I'll make some comments at the start, to welcome everyone. There will be a lot of people coming internationally. And Jo' – his sister, my aunt – 'will say something at the end. And then you and Martin will be in the middle.'

'Martin's talking as well?' Martin, my grandmother's cousin, is a professional historian with a sideline lecturing on cruise liners. Maybe my speech would want more planning than I had thought.

'Yes. They spent the war together in Canada. They've been close ever since. Granny has asked him to speak about their childhood and early years.'

'I see. Symmetry: child, historian, historian, child.'

Only when I got home and told Dierk, my partner, about the plan did I realize the problem. My grandmother has three children. Only two were speaking. My mother was excluded. Perhaps in some families, under some circumstances, this would not be a problem. But relations between my mother and hers have not always been ideal. My parents emigrated to Australia just after my birth and, in the two decades that followed, my aunt and uncle acquired various responsibilities in family affairs that my mother, one hemisphere away, could not, in all practicality, have fulfilled. Yet, in truth, practical considerations in this context merely provide a convenient veneer. The rift – for reasons I do not understand – was deeper.

So, Dierk and I put our heads together to come up with a way of involving my mother. At first, we thought of naming her as co-editor of the booklet of translations and photographs, by then nearing 200 pages, that I was compiling as a surprise for my grand-mother, to be distributed in tandem with the speech at her party. But that felt slightly dubious, *zusammengewürfelt*, in Dierk's words. And adding a fifth speech to the proceedings was unappealing.

Then Dierk hit on the solution: my mother should introduce Martin and me. The suggestion was excellent. Rather than have the two people stand up and speak, in succession but without comment, on overlapping topics, we would have a brief intro-duction, tying our themes together and relating them to my grandmother's interests.

We called my mother – 'How sweet of you both to think of me' – who agreed. All that remained was to broach the subject with my grandmother.

There is no accounting for grandmothers.

The next day, before I had given the matter any further thought, she was on the phone to me. 'The reason I'm calling is that I'm in a quandary about Mummy' – my mother. 'You see, what happened is this. Several people asked if they could make speeches, and it's very kind, but I really don't want too many because even excellent speeches can get dull. So, I thought about you, because of the work you've been doing on the family archive, and Martin, because he's known me so long, and David, to represent the children. But then Jo complained because you're all men and she thinks at least one speaker has to be a woman. And so, I asked her to say something. Now, both David and Jo are speaking and I'm wondering what to do about Mummy.'

'Yes, I see,' I said, and then, with an air of improvisation, produced Dierk's idea.

'Excellent. I'm so glad. You see, I didn't want Mummy to feel left out but I couldn't think how to approach her.' Then a pause. 'But do you think she'd be willing to? I mean, I don't know how she feels about speaking in public.'

'I don't know. Let me call her and ask.' My second lie in as many minutes. 'I'll get back to you after we've spoken.' Technically, not a lie, as the time of my getting back to her would indeed be after the time of my speaking to my mother, even if that had already happened the day before.

I was about to hang up when my grandmother resumed. 'There's one other thing. About the invitations. I thought you might be wondering why I sent you and Dierk separate ones. You see, it's just that . . .' A mild pause. 'I wanted Dierk to know that he was invited. I didn't want him to think that I was inviting you and he was just being allowed to come. I wanted him to know he is invited too.'

This was the second time my grandmother had done this, taken me unawares in regard to her feelings about Dierk and me. The other was shortly after my return from Boston, where I had been studying for five years. During that time, I had been flying back regularly to be with Dierk. Anyone inclined to denial could have regarded this simply as eminent practicality: if one does not like Boston and cannot be bothered to keep apartments there and in London, then, of course, one comes back to London and stays with a friend. When, on my permanent return, Dierk and I moved together into a larger apartment, we did wonder what my grandmother would make of it.

And we decided she would make of it whatever she was comfortable with: if she needed to ignore our relationship, we would let her, but would hope for better.

Then, one day, when I had just begun work on the family archive and we were discussing possible directions, and oatcakes, and the imminence of winter, she said, 'Do you know what I'd really like?' I tried to imagine. To know why the archive had been kept a secret? A recipe for flapjacks? To fly south until springtime? 'I would like you and Dierk to invite me over for lunch.'

The change in topic was so sudden that I did not immediately grasp the significance of what had just been said. When the force of it hit me, I am sure I responded completely inadequately, platitudinously: 'We'd love to', or 'It would be a pleasure', or 'When would you like?'. Something that certainly did not say that I had never been more profoundly touched or moved.

There really is no accounting for grandmothers.

The birthday party arrived. Entering Claridges, the first person I saw was my cousin from the leaving party. I expected the room, already full and loud, to leave Dierk daunted. But before I could reassure him, my aunt Jo, wearing something akin to the Hope diamond, swept him away. In the corner, my brother and his French wife were comparing children with our cousin and his Swiss wife. My other brother was talking with a cousin who, despite just having flown in from Pakistan, wore the air of someone who has just acquired his second polo team. I attempted to return to Dierk with a champagne flute but was waylaid by other cousins; in any event, he was now talking with my Peruvian uncle, probably about gardening or travel, and so would be happy enough.

Lunch was without a table plan. Dierk and I occupied nearby seats and were quickly joined by my mother, one brother and a cousin who opened the conversation with, 'I was in the bathroom earlier when a woman came in and stared at me. I was starting to think she was probably a bit odd but then she said, "Oh, you must be Daniel's sister"!'

Her mother, Jo, passing by, added, 'Yes, because Dil Ara has always complained that she doesn't look like anyone else in the family. But looking at you two now, you really could be brother and sister. Dierk, is that seat by you free? Ah, I'm so glad.' And she and her husband, the Peruvian uncle, joined us.

I am not one for recognizing resemblances. (It is achievement enough for me to recognize my great-grandfather with Lenin when they are pointed out.) However, my aunt had hired a photographer for the afternoon, as a present to her mother. In the resulting photo album, there is a beautiful, spontaneous portrait of me, my 'sister', my brother, and our cousin of the leaving party. Even I am struck by the resemblance. I am just as struck, thumbing through the pages, by the number of portraits that feature Dierk, especially one where my grandmother beams proudly between the two of us.

The speeches go well. My mother's introduction plays on the idea that Martin and I are both family historians, in different senses: me, an historian of the family; Martin, an historian from the family.

I try to give an impression of the scope of the archive, of which, at most, ten per cent has been edited, and draw out some interesting themes. Especially dramatic and well received are the family's near brushes with nonexistence. For instance, my great-grandmother's months in the Black Forest (from where had been sent the registered letter in the orange envelope) had been spent in a sanatorium for lung patients. From this, I had deduced she had suffered from consumption. However, just recently, I had discovered a letter in which she revealed the true cause: a botched

operation had left her with blood poisoning and renal complica-
tions. Yet, by July 1913, she was given the all-clear and allowed to
return home. To be safe, however, she crossed the border into
Switzerland for a second opinion, and some shopping. There,
while waiting for an appointment with the famous Professor
Lahli, she fell by way of another doctor, 'a charlatan', who argued
that she was still ill, gravely ill, with a tumour on the ovaries that
must be operated on at once. She placed her travel plans on hold.

However, once blood-poisoned, twice shy. She waited for a
consultation with Lahli, and then a second, with his former
student, to be sure of the state of her health. This delayed matters
until December 1913. She wrote excitedly to her husband with the
doctor's verdict: 'You can have children', 'Go home, go home.'
She bore her first child, my grandfather, in November 1914.
Evidently, he was conceived a mere two months after the consultation. Had the charlatan been slightly more persuasive, had my
great-grandmother been slightly more trusting, she would have
lost all chance of motherhood there and then. The family line
would have come to an end. The room of people I was addressing
would never have assembled and, in large part, would not even
have existed.

The booklets I had edited had been passed around by this
stage. I explained that they must be read carefully for Communist
connotations, and gave a few examples, building up to Buckie's
discovery of the photograph with Lenin.

Coral, one of my grandmother's oldest friends, approached me
afterwards to make some kind comments and to ask for a copy of
the booklet. 'Of course, that was it, you know.' 'That was what?' I
asked. 'The Communism. That was why Emmanuel kept everything secret.'

The moment she said it, it seemed so obvious. My grandfather
was impeccably English and impeccably capitalist. He had exer-

cised major influence on Thatcher's tax reforms in favour of small and start-up businesses. He had no fondness for the country that had impoverished and attempted to assassinate his parents. The idea that his scrupulously attained position in Britain might be compromised by association with a country and a system that he, in all likelihood, loathed, must have been intolerable to him. Hence, his secrecy.

Families are odd objects. Unlike my great-uncle, I can forgive my grandfather for having lied about the archive he possessed. No two scars are the same. People cope with traumas in different ways. None is wrong. All are regrettable.

During our months spent working in the archive room, me telling my grandmother of the latest discoveries, her corroborating with old stories and rumours, our relationship has changed. In addition to our being grandparent and grandchild, we are collaborators, co-explorers, her discovering her in-laws, me discovering my forebears. I regret that my grandfather did not permit anyone to have a similar relationship with him.

Work on the archive, especially since publication of the first booklet, has galvanized the family. New letters are emerging. New contacts are being formed. The archive, if he could have shared it, at least in his later years, would have enriched, not endangered, my grandfather's happiness. Instead, the time he spent with the archive was time spent in isolation, recording on the back of photographs the names of faces only he recognized, reidentifying the curves and angles of handwriting that only he recalled: a photograph of his father's best friend, his grandfather's obituary, a letter informing of his great-grandfather's death. I regret that he did all this alone.

And, when I reflect on my family, I regret that our society – a union of decent people, who care about human difference and human dignity – has allowed 'family values' to become a weapon of bigots. I have no doubt, not a sliver, not a scintilla, that Dierk and I are valued by our family just as much as we value them. And yet, the family-values lobby broadcasts the lie that our love endangers our family. In reality, families are at risk only from their closed-mindedness, which condemns and pares off children, siblings, parents, cousins. It is true that homosexuals do not form nuclear units of father–mother–kids. But such hermetic units are not what families are about. Real families stretch across generations, continents and languages. They include grandparents, cousins and cousins' cousins. And such extended families extend to homosexuals. When the 'family values' lobby pretends otherwise, they reveal a sad misvaluing of family life. We must never lose sight of the truth. We must never allow them to claim the moral high ground or to lecture down to us.

Helen Munro

I probably came out to myself when I was about 13 or 14 years old. The acknowledgement of sexuality came fairly early on. What helped was that it was a time when there were a lot of gay characters on television, particularly the soaps *Emmerdale* and *EastEnders*. Also in the early 1990s, a couple of films came out, particularly *Basic Instinct* (2002) where Sharon Stone plays a bisexual character. Then I came out to my friends and my family when I was about 16, at the beginning of my A-levels, and it was never an issue.

From the age of about 16, I guess, I started going out into Soho, and I went to a place called London Friend, which I believe still exists, up on Caledonian Road. I found that through the wonders of *Time Out*. Everyone there was considerably older than me. I made a few friends, I started going out drinking in a few bars in Leicester Square, and I went to the main lesbian event of the time, 'Venus Rising', which was a *huge* monthly night out in Brixton. And then after about six or nine months of doing that, I told one of my best friends and she was totally fine. A few other people found out, and then while we were doing our A-levels some friends would come to gay clubs and bars with me. And they quite enjoyed it. It was definitely different from south-east London.

Were you surprised by how easy it all was?
I certainly wouldn't have expected my friends to be horrified. I told my dad when I was about 16 or 17, and the reason was that at weekends he didn't know where I was or where I was going, which was bizarre and unsafe. I thought I should let my parents

know what I was doing with my life, so that's why I told him. I was actually very, very nervous about telling him. I had some Dutch courage before I did so, but he was just great, he said, 'I didn't know anyone gay before, but now I do', and we didn't discuss it. I don't think we've ever really discussed it, but he accepts that's me, that's my life, and that's fine. My mum, too, was absolutely fine with it.

Just to backtrack a little, did you find the provision of sex education at school adequate, or did you find it left you feeling rather confused?
I have to say, I don't remember one sex education class, except maybe putting a condom on a carrot, that sort of thing. I'm sure we had videos about certain STIs. It was still the era of HIV and AIDS and that's what the overarching concern was about: disease, fear and caution. I don't want this to be construed in the wrong way, but by the time they came round to giving us sex education we had probably educated ourselves. So I don't think it mattered, actually. Obviously, lots of homophobic comments were flung around at school, and still are – not that they were ever directed towards me, more towards the young men.

I was pretty opinionated then, as I am now. There were plenty of other kids to pick on rather than me, and I'd have been quite a hard battle to win. A couple of guys were gay who weren't openly out, they got an awful lot of stick. I didn't avoid 'stick' – I tried to engage in 'debates' about sexuality.

So from school to university, was that a fairly neat transition in terms of self-expression, or was it a liberating experience?
No, not at all, because I was out to anyone that I could have possibly been out to, and I had a girlfriend when I went to university. No, it was fine. I can't say that I wasn't anxious – one always is. I was going to live away from home for the first time

and live with eight people, sharing one bathroom, in a very, very small, confined space. I remember turning up on the first day and looking through the list of people whom I was to share my flat with, and there was one from Paignton, in the West Country, and I thought it was going to be absolutely awful. He turned out to be one of my best friends, and still is now. I told him within about half an hour that I was gay, in the pub on the first night. Most of the issues I had came from people from the south east, and young women who didn't quite understand what it was to be a lesbian, which made me challenge my own preconceptions about people in general.

I had very mixed acquaintances, largely because I fancied all the straight girls. I was chair of the lesbian, gay and bisexual society in my second year, and I was part of that all my university career. I very much enjoyed that, and my friend and I tried to organize it, because when we signed up it consisted of going down to the pub on a Thursday night and getting pissed. That was great, because for lots of people who were coming out, or who had come out, it was all a bit too much to sit around and talk about anything political. But we organized roadshows, linked up with the HIV/AIDS education group and did some work with them, and had some open forums. That's probably the most active on gay issues that I've ever been. But the drive and the desire to continue just weren't there, other members were happy just to go down the pub, and on bar trips into Brighton – and of course that has its place.

Presumably Brighton's a great place in which to be a gay student
I chose Brighton because of the course, and only subsequently found out about the gay life. When I decided I was going to go there I went down to Brighton Pride, when I was 17, about 1992 or 1993, and it's phenomenal how things have changed since then.

It was only about 100 people marching through Brighton, so it's moved on incredibly in the past ten years or so.

After graduating, I stayed on in Brighton, and worked for Brighton and Hove Council for just under a year. I wouldn't be able to tell you if I came out during that time because I wasn't friends with anyone at work. I'm sure I probably would have told people that I spoke to. Then I came home and did a masters degree at the London School of Economics for nine months; it was very intense, about the hardest work I've ever done in my entire life. I went from there to the Department of the Environment for 18 months or so, then into consultancy.

Have you ever been a member of any LGBT organizations, formal or informal, in the workplace?
I am sure that there is a LGBT organization in the civil service but I never sought it out and was never made aware of it. I have never consciously tried to demarcate my personal and professional lives.

One of the things that drives me is that I genuinely have no issues with my sexuality. I enjoy it and I like it. When you meet people who do have a particular problem with your sexuality, there's nothing for them to pick at, there's no vulnerable gap where they can say, 'That's where she feels weak.' What stops me feeling optimistic, and where I become very pessimistic, are the experiences of other people I know, which remind me that being gay *is* a challenge still, for certain people.

In terms of the experience I had with my family, I'm an exception. I've also worked for my company for five years, and everyone knows my sexuality; I socialize with people in my age group. I only told my boss fairly recently – but only because I didn't socialize with him before that.

*You work for a parliamentary lobbyist. I imagine that involves moving
in a macho, political society . . .*
I think if I were to socialize more with the peers in my profession,
I probably would struggle. Maybe that's the reason why I don't.
It's a boyish profession and not particularly forgiving. It's hugely
competitive. Mind you, if I went to a social event and met a
director of another organization who was homophobic, I think
that rather than shying away from it I'd probably face it.

*Have you been conscious of a changing climate outside your own
experience in terms of gay rights? I was going to come on to the Civil
Partnership Act; I don't know if it has benefited you in any way,
or whether you have taken advantage of any of its provisions?*
No, it hasn't affected me and I haven't taken advantage of any of
its provisions, although that doesn't mean I won't in the future.
The value of it? It's a chicken-and-egg case. Do you have a
cultural shift followed by a legal shift, or a legal shift followed by
a cultural shift? I don't mean to sound defeatist or apathetic, but
it's the same when we could have had equal age of consent at 16.
The gay community acts these things out regardless of whether
the law says they can do it or not. The question is: why do we
need the convention to allow us? I understand that in terms of tax
or inheritance, the Act is important – they are functions of living.
But I'm not too sure a subculture that lives different lives requires
convention from the law. I don't actually think that it helps a
cultural shift, or what people think about whether I should be
allowed to hold hands with my girlfriend or not, and whether
they should be able to shout abuse at me. Although, that said, the
media coverage on gay unions has so far been very positive and
will hopefully assist in moving attitudes forward.

　　We've been allowed a space within society at the moment,
which is fine, but just the fact that you're allowed a space pisses

me off enough not to want to be a part of it. There may be a time, maybe for my grandchildren, when that space is no longer a space and it's truly merged, but at the moment it's 'concessions', and it's 'tolerance', and that in itself is ridiculous. Going back to what you said about being fortunate for never having had anyone criticize me or question my sexuality, I mean that's absolutely ridiculous. Why should I be fortunate, why should I be grateful, why should I be appreciative that somebody accepts me? I'm not a radical person generally, but I think I probably am in my sexual politics.

Speaking very generally, do you see any negative aspects of sexuality in the workplace, such as the development of a 'gay mafia', or events that possibly ghettoize gay men and women?
There are networking opportunities for women, but it always ends up being a piss-up. I don't really mind, I don't have a passionate view on that at all. I think the gay community these days does a very good job of ghettoizing itself as well as being ghettoized and I quite like the fact that there's a difference. As long as there is a bridge to communicate ideas from one side to the other, so that we don't detach ourselves. The ultimate goal is to move closer, not to drift further apart, but I don't think we're ready to merge just yet.

I don't go out in Soho as much as I used to – that's to do with being in a relationship, I guess – but I've grown up going to Soho, and, you know, you turn into Old Compton Street or Wardour Street and your shoulders relax and you're in your haven – I still get excited about that and love that. I go there with straight friends as well as my gay friends. I don't want it to be exclusive at all, but nor do I want to see it watered down. Everybody likes to feel that they can go somewhere because of who they are, and that distinguishes them from the ever more homogenized society that we live in. You know, we've been Starbucked, so I'd really like to go to Balans.

Where do see yourself and the gay rights situation ten or twenty years from now?
It's only ever going to move in the right direction. I think the media are hugely important. At present, it is often a negative role, and not just over-identifying with people who are gay, but also over issues such as Catholic priests who have been abusing young boys. That's seen as a gay issue and not as a sexual predator issue. That's a slight distraction. But the media doesn't qualify what it says or make distinctions. This goes full circle in the conversation, but I think the fact that there are lots of gay characters on TV, or that shows have gay characters in them, is hugely important. If there were more pop stars, politicians, TV presenters, high-profile environmentalists – whoever, whatever is your bag – who allowed their sexuality to be made open if they were gay, I think that would be one of the most helpful things.

I think the issue with the media is whether gay people are brave enough to come out, and whether they will be treated with respect and dignity or whether they're going to try and humiliate them, depending on the readership. I don't think the *Sun* is ever going to promote gay rights. Maybe if it would, it would up the ante. I'm no expert on the media or PR or marketing, but from my perspective I think the media could play a fantastic role. At the TV awards recently, the Best New Actor was the gay actor from *Coronation Street*, Anthony Cotton. In his 'thank you' speech, he said, 'This is so important having a gay character in *Coronation Street*', and I thought that was great. But soaps tend to rotate, so one has a gay character for about six months, then another has one for another six months, and there is little consistency.

In my personal life I would say that I am settled. I definitely would like children but that's a real pickle of a situation, I don't know how that would happen. I'd like some dogs but no cats. Preferably not a Volvo either. Definitely living in London.

Do you think your experience would have been different outside of London and the south east?
I think my school experience would probably have been the same. I mean I didn't get much hassle. I don't believe that anyone needs to be a hero wherever they are, I certainly don't do enough, I think, for the things that I believe in – but if people don't take a few small steps regardless of who or where they are, we remain at a standstill.

Credit: Grant Hiroshima

Stephen Hough

If I may use this quaint euphemism, whispered in the late Victorian years when even homophobia dare not speak its name, I actually did know I was 'musical' before I knew I was musical. From the age of four onwards I was deeply, vitally aware that I was attracted emotionally and romantically to boys rather than girls. Of course the explicitly sexual dimension of such an attraction came later, but I knew, when it did come, that it was a branch sprouting from the same root which in turn had grown from a seed at the oldest, deepest part of my being.

It is strange looking back at those childhood years where memories are muddled like crumpled papers at the back of musty drawers. I had no traumatic experiences – no dead spiders – but I did share with most homosexual children growing up at that time (mid-1960s) a strange instinct for survival that meant hiding, denying, pretending, and hoping that somehow it could be different. The delicate awakening of tenderness, before 'homosexual' was a word known or pronounced, had to be crushed in the panic of recognition – waking into a nightmare rather than out of one. It really was like pulling the flower out of the ground as it bloomed, the torn roots remaining deep in the soil.

One of my greatest fears in early life was that I would be discovered to be gay – by friends, neighbours, teachers or relatives. It was a fear which grew as I grew, and as I felt the sting of playground jokes and savoured the stale, sour comments of grown-ups. It was like holding on to a terrible secret: an insect captured inside a jam-jar where the lid could come off at any moment. The default setting in society at that time was that in revelation one faced rejection. It is still the case in many parts of the world today. Silence is death: but speech is worse. Where most parents plan and wait impatiently for their children's wedding day, for the same parents the revelation that a son or daughter is gay can mean an end to communication, a banning from the home, an erasing from the family. The gay child can find that he or she has lost *two* families: the parental home and the chance to form a future relationship protected and nurtured by society.

The first message of explicit negativity I heard towards being gay came from my religious beliefs as I entered my teenage years in an evangelical church. The teaching was that something growing within me (which *was* me) was disgusting and must be kept quiet, cured, squashed, punished . . . anything will do. Reading my Bible I would fear opening the scorching pages of Romans 1 or 1 Corinthians 6. These brief passages shine with a terrible light for a gay person, until we look at what they aim to illumine rather than at the light itself. Just as we can now see clearly the inadequacy of St Paul's teaching on women or slavery and excuse his historical limitations, so we need not blame him for his lack of understanding of the concept of same-sex love. He was looking through a window at first-century Rome and Corinth with first-century Jewish eyes from a perspective of religious and cultural separation which had lasted for centuries. It is highly unlikely that he saw gay couples in faithful, committed partnerships; and it is certain that he saw all kinds of orgiastic, abusive behaviour which would often have been linked to pagan rites and beliefs. What else could he have written in his situation?

I became a Catholic at the age of 19 and the teaching on homosexuality remained the same, although being unmarried now became a respectable, even glamorous option. Priests, nuns and monks were all able to live safely without the enquiries: 'Why aren't you married?', 'Have you got a girlfriend?' I even considered the priesthood myself, partly to avoid having to answer honestly such terrifying questions. Yet I remained a musician, accepting the Church's prohibition, buried under my work, avoiding 'occasions of sin', destroying certain friendships before there was any chance of them developing into anything intimate – in many ways a happy yet somehow shrunken life.

It was when reading Pope John Paul II's famous book *Love and Responsibility*, published in 1960 when he was an auxiliary bishop in Krakow, that I first began to think again about this issue. You cannot offer such a radiant and dazzling vision of love and human relationships to your readers, and then exclude those who happen to have 'green eyes'. Once you have affirmed, as he did controversially and courageously for a Catholic bishop of his time, the sacredness of the human body and its self-gift in the sexual act you have opened a floodgate of recognition for all who have both bodies to reverence and 'selves' to give. 'It is not good that the man should be alone', said God in the opening chapters of the Bible and of human history – the one blemish in an otherwise unblemished world, where everything was 'very good'. Such an affirmation of companionship at the beginning of time is fresh and inspiring still; and, combined with new discoveries about sexual orientation in the natural world, it opens up a radical challenge to previously confident assessments of the morality of gay relationships.

To share a life of intimacy with another is the way the vast majority of men and women, regardless of their gender preference, are meant to live whole and holy lives. Such relationships are about more than making babies. They are about making love, because to do so is to be fully human, with sensitive, 'musical' hearts attuned to vibrations which animals may hear but only men and women can hold. Celibacy is only of value as an affirmation of what is renounced – the best given up freely because it is the best gift one can give. If celibacy is not rare, and a totally free donation, it has the whiff of something slightly perverse about it – literally 'contrary to nature'.

We are subject to natural law as part of creation, but we are also able to contemplate it and relish it. It is the great epiphany of reality: what is actually there, not what we would like to be there, or what our forebears have told us is there. It can be full of surprises, and it has no favourites. The one who confidently claims natural law as an ally in arguing for the sanctity of life might end up finding it an annoying foe in a discussion on homosexuality. When the world in which we live tells a different story from what we were taught, we eventually have to break free. It isn't so much that law changes, but that the Church (from St Paul onwards) simply has not had the vocabulary to discuss an issue it neither named nor understood. (The idea that a person could actually *be* homosexual, rather than a badly behaved heterosexual, has only been accepted by the Catholic Church in the past 30 years or so.)

Law is living and flexible: always growing, adapting, changing shape; never abandoning its roots but never rigid either. Christ not only boiled theology down to the simple statement: 'God is love', he also distilled the complex religious laws of his time to love of that same God and of neighbour as oneself. The spiritual liberty and simplicity which resulted from this new, unified vision led, in theory at least, to the breaking down of the divisive barriers between men and women, slave and free, Jew and Gentile. It is tragic that it took Christians at least 1,900 years even to begin to explore or live this freedom in practice. The prison gates were open but we remained inside, either cowering in the corner or standing with arms outstretched, blocking the exit. Both responses came from fear, and both were betrayals of the Christian message.

Ultimately the only real argument against homosexual equality is a belief that God has told us it is wrong. All the other reasons given (destruction of the family, seduction of the young, unnatural behaviour, a genetic disorder like alcoholism) are attempts to find a common, secular currency to barter for what is an *a priori*, religious judgement. But the coins are fake and are being rendered obsolete by common sense and daily experience. Actually I believe that the religious arguments are wrong too, and that, as with slavery, the churches will have to re-evaluate their teaching on this issue – but that's for another chapter, indeed another book! That re-evaluation will probably take decades, but in the meantime the churches cannot expect gay non-Christians in a secular world to abstain from sexual relationships from their teenage years up to the end of their lives; and thus they cannot exclude those same people from either marriage or a formal, legal commitment and then complain that such relationships are unstable. Straight couples are no strangers to marital collapse, even with the cement of children and society's affirmation to encourage them to hold firm, so why should we expect even higher standards from gays?

To use 'musical' as a euphemism for homosexual is rather flattering when you think about it. It suggests a sensitivity, a creativity, an ability to attune to sound and beauty. Of course it was originally an ironic, snide use of the term: a real man might whistle *at* work, or bawl a song in the pub *after* work, but to be touched or moved by music below the surface seemed weak, lacking in moral fibre of that tough, fearless type which was the male ideal. It is not an accident that music and the arts were always a tolerant environment for gay men. It was a world where an appreciation of the 'feminine' was not seen as weakness, and where strength did not have to manifest itself in violence and coarseness. (It also became a safe place for gay people to hide and to flourish among like-minded friends in the years – not that long ago – when blackmail and prison were an ever-possible threat.) But perhaps we can go even further. The modern performing artist is really a direct descendant of the village entertainer, found in the earliest human communities. This person, at least while on-stage, was an outsider, someone disguised or different, looked upon with admiration and envy, or even fear and discomfort as he transported his audience to realms of fantasy, amusement or glamour, away from the mundane and humdrum. The entertainment involved could be singing, dancing, acting, conjuring, story-telling . . . a whole host of different things. It was the perfect place in which to indulge a sense of the extravagant and exuberant, as well as offering ideal camouflage. A mask, a costume, an affecting melody, a graceful leap were all perfect alibis for those whose affections danced to a different tune – a Scheherazade-like escape from the 1,001 knights in the community ready to pronounce and enact the death sentence. If the gay artist could hold the audience captive he might avoid being captured himself.

All of this is not to suggest that gay people are inherently more sensitive or artistic than straights (notwithstanding the famous pianist Vladimir Horowitz's mischievous statement that there are three kinds of pianists: Jewish, homosexual and bad!); but everyone draws on a central emotional core in the act of creativity, and when the normal outlet of intimacy is blocked, the heart will find alternative ways to express itself, sometimes with enormous intensity. At best, art can become a fountain quenching an inner, passionate thirst; at worst, it is a form of sheer survival – galoshes against the puddles.

I was certainly aware, from an early age, that the physical and emotional reflexes in playing the piano were a uniquely satisfying form of self-expression. In front of the keyboard was a place of legitimate release, and music became a secret, wordless language in which to speak or sing freely and fervently. In front of an audience now, as a professional pianist, such communication is public, yet strangely liberating. I delight to play, as if intimately and in confidence, for every individual person in every seat in the hall.

*　　*　　*

Epiphanies occur in many areas of human life – in science, in culture, and in morality. Only 50 years ago many American states continued to enforce laws which maintained the superiority of whites over blacks. A hundred years earlier than that, blacks had no rights whatsoever in those same states. How could such abuses have been promoted, accepted and justified for so long? Tragically, much blood was shed and wars fought before minds were prepared to make the radical changes required. There has been a huge leap forward for gay rights over the last 50 years, but what alchemy is needed now for the final steps towards full equality? In the West gay people are no longer thrown into prison, but often can merely be tolerated rather than accepted: no longer persecuted, but not celebrated either; greeted with a smile, but not yet an embrace; given food, but not a feast.

We are standing at a unique gateway as we enter the twenty-first century. There has been an increasing impatience with the lying and loneliness of the closet, and gay people are finding a new vocabulary of love and confidence. They want to commit themselves to each other in mature, stable partnerships. Not being the 'marrying kind' is no longer a sufficient excuse for iso-lation. The eccentric bachelor-uncles and spinster-aunts are not content any more to be guests at other people's homes: they want to host parties with their own families – and what fun parties they turn out to be!

The floodgates are open, but we find that the water is good; we can swim, we needn't fear, we can embrace and be embraced by the waves. People are realizing increasingly that their best friends, their children's best friends, their neighbours and colleagues, their politicians and admired public figures are gay. Gay liberation will have arrived when, as a term and concept, it has become archaic. That will be the point when understanding and tolerance have been transformed into the familiarity of friendship – that love which has no need to speak its name.